WHY IT'S NOT ENOUGH TO 'JUST' BE AN ACTOR IN THE 21ST CENTURY

SAMUELL BENTA

Disclaimer

This book offers no guarantee of success; success depends upon the individual's attitude, perseverance, and attentiveness to detail. This book is a means of sharing information that has helped the author himself.

ISBN: 978-0-9955925-0-6

Contents

PART 1

Introduction

YOU ARE A DIAMOND

It is no accident that you are reading this book. Something drew you to it; there was an inward curiosity that made you want to find out information on why it's not enough to *just* be an actor in the 21st century. Whatever the reason, if you look deep enough into the contents of this book you will find a secret, not about acting, but life. Isn't that what acting is about? Life, and living the lives of other characters and people? I don't know who you are that is reading these lines; you may be an up and coming actor, an actor that's done a few gigs or a seasoned actor. Either way, it doesn't matter. I want to have a conversation with you as everything I mention in this book is relevant to any stage you are at in your career.

First, it would help if you knew more about me, Samuell Benta. I started off acting when I was very young, but took things more professionally when I was 17 years old. Before this, I wasn't really doing much. I had attended college doing a BTEC course on Music Technology, and that was only because I wanted to do a fun subject. During these times, my cousin starred on a TV soap called 'Hollyoaks', and after seeing her on the TV, it made me want to be on TV. It may sound ridiculous but this was what I wanted. The age of 19 was when I landed my first gig on TV, which was only a few lines in a popular TV show in the UK called *'The Bill'*. Like most of you, I had found an agent, went for auditions, and eventually got the part for something. There was a period of two years where I had no acting work before my first gig came around. It was endless auditions before that, *and that was if I even had the chance to get in a casting director's room*. I remember my very first audition. It was for a play called *'Little Sweet Thing'* by Roy Williams when I was in my late teens. I didn't get the part, though, but I will never forget my first audition.

As time went by, I landed more roles, more for TV than anything, but then it got to a stage where I noticed something wasn't right. Any actor will know that we hate when a gig ends because we never know when the next one is going to be. Acting isn't a 9-5 job, although we wish it were because we would always be regularly working doing something we love, and getting paid for it. Most actors work normal jobs during the day, and find the time to get off work to go to auditions. Does this sound like you? I personally hated this routine of waiting for the next gig. I take my life seriously because time is precious, and I know some of you may be thinking *'yeah, but that's how it is'*. Yes, that's understandable, but times have changed over the years.

Once upon a time, actors never had the internet, never had devices with social media, never had YouTube or Instagram.

Tracking back and connecting the dots, I have been able to witness the changes take place not just by being an actor, but by producing, writing, and directing as well. I have been on all sides of the spectrum to see the shifts that have taken place for things to be a lot simpler for actors, but also a lot harder...

Before I continue, I just want to let you know that acting is an amazing field, and I don't regret any work that I have done and neither should you yours, because it has led me to where I am today to share this message with you. As you read this book you will come to the realisation that 'acting' is not enough to make it to the top in this new digital age that we live in. The rise of Netflix, Amazon, and social media has totally changed the game of how decisions are being made, by the people who choose to employ YOU! As actors, unfortunately they do not see the decision-making process. I, however, have evolved to be able to witness what happens behind the scenes, and find out what gives that actor that extra factor that gets them booked.

Before becoming booked there needs to be an awareness about who you are. Ask yourself, what does this person bring to the table? You reader, are a multidimensional being, a diamond with many sides. If you are a diamond, then why only show one side of yourself? I empathise because what you are about to read is not what the average drama school, casting director or other actor will share with you, because they themselves do not know what it *really* takes to succeed. Acting is one sided, it's only one side of the diamond that you already are.

Bill Gates[1] said that no one gets to vote whether technology is going to change our lives... this is true! Look at how addicted you are to your phone: updating statuses, taking selfies, tweeting, putting pics on Instagram, snapchatting, accessing emails from your phone on the go - it never used to be like this! Technology has also changed the *behaviours* of the *decision-making process* of people in the entertainment industry as well. With so much content to consume from video on demand, actors can get lost if they don't build themselves up. Actors need to keep up with the tide with the way the wind is blowing, or they will get lost in the competition. I am happy that you have come across this book, and I hope it helps you to build a bigger picture of yourself, so you can realise what a diamond you really are, no matter how rough your circumstances may be. Relax, take a seat, and learn, 'why it's NOT ENOUGH to *just* be an ACTOR in the 21st Century'.

---

[1] Bill Gates "The Road Ahead" Viking. 1995

CHAPTER 1

POLITICS AND THE INDUSTRY

Over the course of this book, you will be taken on a 7-year journey where you will find out why the title is so true. I want to share with you my story of where I started, and how things evolved from being dissatisfied to transforming my life.

As a black actor, I had done quite well with the shows that were being credited to my IMDB profile, but you get tired of waiting around for your agent to call you up with auditions, and I knew I wanted more from life. I wanted to have something I could call mine, something I created which would give opportunities to other actors as well as help boost my name in the industry. Just because I had a few jobs on my CV, didn't necessarily mean roles were being offered. *I can get very political talking about the following...* but with the UK in general, we don't get a lot of black shows on TV, and if we do they will all be one of the five below:

1) Cast that have been used time and time again so we see the same faces
2) Negative portrayals, showing a black person doing something *'wrong'* in society
3) A token black cast member amongst a predominantly white cast
4) An American show which has a lot of black cast members that was acquired by a UK TV network
5) An American show with a black British actor who flew out the country because there was no *'proper'* roles being created in their own

You can guarantee we will always see a rerun of 'Fresh Prince of Bel Air, *which is now on Netflix'.* I personally love the show, but the point I am trying to make is that it's not 'British'. It's always American shows with black actors, and never British shows with black actors. I remember years ago, we had a channel called *'Trouble',* which had an unlimited amount of content catered towards the black community. They had programs such as *'Fresh Prince of Bel Air', 'The Wayans Brothers', 'Moesha', 'Sister Sister', 'Eve', 'All of Us', 'Malcom and Eddie', 'Smart Guy', 'Hanging with Mr Cooper'* and many more. You, the reader, may be smiling as you have just pictured these shows in your mind as it brought back sweet memories as a child, *depending on your age of course.*

I want you to look at those titles and ask yourselves, which of those shows were British -NONE! I am not against American shows; I'm just clearly making a point that we have grown up to love and watch American content with no idea of our own identities. The only black shows we have had in the UK were *'No Problem (1983)', 'Desmonds (1989-1994)', 'Brothers and Sisters (1996)' which doesn't even show any history online! 'The Real McKoy (1991-1996)' and 'The Crouches (2003-2005)'*. All these shows were great within their own right; however, 'The Crouches' had a white writer! Do I hear alarm bells ringing? I don't want to delve too deep into this, but it always felt like there was *'something'* controlling *'our'* stories. 'The Crouches' ended after two series and it wasn't particular loved by the audience for various, and personally, I might add *'obvious'* reasons.

Trouble TV was closed in 2003 which was a major loss to the generation at the time, in terms of black content which we could relate to and enjoy. There was a loss in entertainment and we were fed whatever was given to us after that time. I researched online, and saw blogs from various people asking questions and even sending letters to networks asking what happened to all the black sitcoms and shows in general. Surprise, surprise, there was no response, so I remained a fly on the wall and observed what was happening on TV, and I didn't like what I saw. You may possibly agree with the statement *'it always comes down to the money and what sells!'*

As a young black rising actor, I had to ask myself, where's the hope of getting better roles other than the stereotype estate, gang, drug, guns type of characters? I was sick of it and so frustrated with the industry as a whole. My agent even said to me, *"You need to play the game in this industry"* my reply was, *"not if you have integrity and believe that what is portrayed consistently is what people will believe"*. I mean this on a deep subconscious spiritual level. It showed me a side of my agent or agents in general, that it always comes down to the money and what sells, there's no real, personal value system of morals or ethics taken into consideration with this industry.

You hear stories of black actors flying out to the states, such as Idris Elba, Lennie James and David Harewood, who are doing extremely well across the Atlantic. The roles they have had there, you would never see in the UK, so ask yourself what does this do to the psyche of the black actor in the UK? What does this do to the psyche of the black person in the UK? Some of us believe there's no hope, some of us just accept whatever roles there are because we're desperate, but I refused, because I believe we are great people and deserve the best! Yes, you can be sure that I have rejected so many auditions because of the repetitiveness of the same *'quality'* of roles, even to the extent of my agent wanting to get rid of me, but I didn't let that stop my integrity, my blood was boiling and I had an organic sense of urgency to change things not just for my life but for the whole human race. It was December 2010, and I declared myself a man on a Mission.

CHAPTER 2

MAN ON A MISSION

In the next few chapters, I will be telling you my story. I think it's worth knowing my background and the bigger picture, so you can see it for yourself. After reading this book, I hope you will have a whole new realisation on your outlook not just in this industry, but on life and your responsibility.

Fuelled by my frustration and desire to change things, I had an idea - I wanted to create my own TV show. I had never done it before, but I knew I wanted to do it. I woke up one morning and I said to my little brother I wanted to create my own show. I didn't know what it was going to be about, but I wanted it to be funny. He told me I should do it, but I had no idea how to start. The next day I paid a visit to my friend and we sat down with a sheet of paper for brainstorming. I was clueless as to what to start with, so he said I should write a show about my life. *At the time, I was going through a rough relationship with my partner involving my daughter, who was 1 years old.* I remember remaining silent and thought it would be a great idea. After a couple of hours brainstorming, I left confident knowing that with the notes we came up with, I could come up with A few characters.

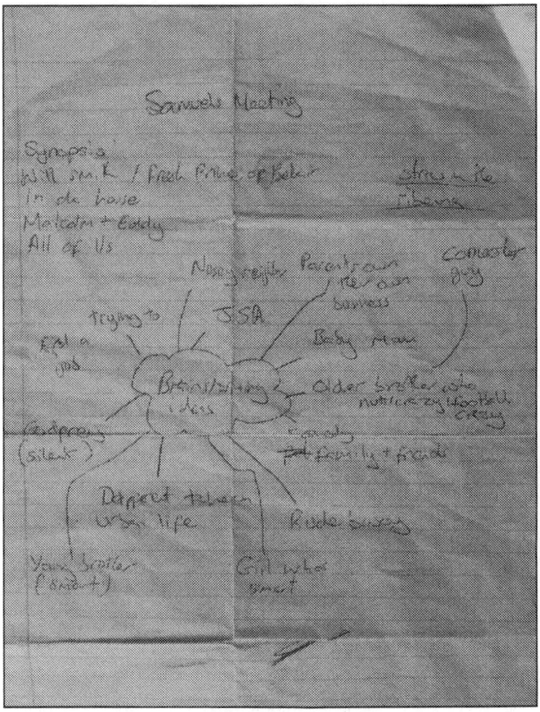

(The original 'All About the McKenzies' brainstorm 2010.)

I wrote down a goal, and said by April 21st 2011, I would be in production. I didn't know how but that was my goal, which meant I had about four months to get myself to that position. I had something to work towards. My inspirations were

American shows such as *The Fresh Prince of Bel Air, My Wife and Kids,* and *Martin.* I knew my show had to be a hit, and it had to be great. All I needed was a great script and great cast, but I was unaware of how to go about doing it.

One thing I can say I am very grateful for is the internet, because you can find anything you want on there. I was researching how to go about writing a script professionally, because I did not want to write it on Microsoft word. *My whole attitude was to do everything to the best of my ability,* so I looked up scripts from shows that had already aired to see how the layout of their script was. I remember looking at a script for US Sitcom *'Frasier'* and *'Girlfriends'*. They were all different layouts but I knew I had to start somewhere, so I chose one layout and began searching for some free scriptwriting software. *For those of you who are interested in writing there is a software for scriptwriting called Celtix It's amazing! YouTube is great as there are video tutorials for everything*; I watched a short five-minute tutorial on how to use Celtix, and I was ready to go.

Starting off a story was such a challenge and I was having trouble. For a week, nothing had been written and I was very concerned. How on Earth could I start off writing a show?

One evening, I was on the bus on my way to a seminar, my brother texted me. He said my friend Ian had texted him asking me to call him. I called Ian, we had a chat and he told me he was writing a script for his friend. I had known Ian for years but never knew he wrote scripts. We arranged to meet up one day so he could see where I was at with my idea. After spending, a few hours with him, we had come up with a plan for the first episode. I got straight to writing, and about a week later I had written the first episode, which aimed to be twenty-two minutes long. Thinking of a name for the show took a while. You may be wondering how I came up with it. I was pondering for ages after the script was written and there was a song that popped into my head. It was an old Puff Daddy song called *'All About The Benjamins'*. This was a light-bulb moment, and I had a thought to myself, which was to change Benjamins to a completely different name. I went through all the names I could think of, and decided to use McKenzies! Funny, huh? So, script completed and a title for the show – done. The question was, now what? What was the next step? I didn't know.

A week later, I attended another seminar to see what was going on in social media. Someone approached me having recognised my face and introduced himself to me. He asked me if I knew someone by the name of Tony Adez, to which I replied *"yes". (Tony was a long-time friend of mine who used to record my music; sadly, he's no longer with us).* We got talking and he told me he had seen Tony editing my show-reel years ago - *that's how he remembered my face*. We exchanged details and I told him about what I was doing. He had a look at my script and told me what I needed was a plan for future episodes. This was what I was lacking, a plan of how the show will pan out for the first series! I was meant to meet this person to show me the next step in the process.

I woke up one morning and was inspired by a thought to do a video presentation of my idea and put it online. This was so random, but I had an impression to take action on this presentation. *I personally love doing video presentations they are fun.* I thought this would be a great opportunity to let people know what I was doing and hopefully attract people who wanted to get involved. Without wasting anytime, I got out my laptop and loaded up PowerPoint thinking carefully about how to construct the necessary slides explaining in detail what I was looking to do. As we think in pictures, it was wise to use pictures in the presentation, so after looking at images on Google, I found pictures of how I visualised the characters. I learnt how to use Adobe Photoshop to cut out the people in the pictures and combine them together, *through a lot of trial and error of course*. After successfully completing this I knew that I wanted to record my voice narrating the presentation. I downloaded a free screen recording software and recorded myself talking about the project stating at the end of the presentation the type of people I was looking for, and put my contact details on there.

(A slide from the presentation March 2011 I put online, for security I have # the details)

A very spooky thing happened, the moment I had completed the presentation, my phone rang. It was the guy I met at the seminar! He asked me where I was at with my show and I told him about the presentation. He then suggested I post it on a website called filmakersunited.com. Using my intuition, I went along with it. Twenty-four hours later, a woman contacted me on the site telling me my idea was very interesting. I had a look at her profile and saw a link to a website called starnow.co.uk. I never knew what this was, but after some research I discovered I could post on their site for free. After posting it on the website, I had people contacting me every day via phone, email and Facebook wanting to get involved. In total, I had over 10,000 views and over 500 applications in the space of 4 weeks - I was so overwhelmed! People wanted to write, direct and act in the show. *I just want the reader to take a mental note that, originally, I wasn't supposed to be the director or producer.*

When I posted online, my intention was to look for people who wanted to help me and experience the making of the show. I had posted I was looking for writers, actors, directors, producers, and investors. No investors had contacted me even though I contacted them, but I didn't let that stop me as I had to keep moving forward. Through these contacts a lovely woman called Simone contacted me on Facebook. She was very talented and had great experience in production. She had worked for a television company and she knew how to link characters, their relationships and create episodic ideas. She surprised me when we met in Starbucks in Ealing Broadway by showing me stuff she had written. The presentation I did was extremely comprehensive. She automatically connected with these characters. After a couple of weeks of knowing her I told her she was going to have a higher role in this whole production. We decided it would be best for us to work on a three-minute teaser which we could send around to different TV companies with a treatment and proposal.

A young writer from South London contacted me saying she wanted to be a writer for the show. I will not mention her name here, but for the purpose of this book, I will call her Denise. She was eighteen years old and was fired up to be involved in the process. She helped write an episode and this girl was brilliant! She too connected with the characters and brought a youthful aspect to the project. The decision was to make 8x22 minute episodes. We planned and decided I would write the 1st, 3rd, 5th, 7th episode and she would write the 2nd, 4th, 6th and we would both collaborate on the 8th. An unfortunate thing happened - Denise went AWOL. I never heard from her again, and wasn't able to get through to her phone. I never let that stop me. I kept on going and decided I would write the eight episodes myself. What happened was that as time was getting on I had to keep asking Denise for the third episode so I could move on. I knew she had college and had started a drama school, and I must have pestered her too much, which resulted in her switching off on me. I forgave myself, took responsibility and continued. A lesson to be learned.

A lady from West London called Carolyn emailed me showing her interest as a production assistant. I found her approach intriguing when I met her. She shared information I had never experienced before when she spoke about areas of the industry that I had no knowledge of. Through Carolyn, I met her friend John, who had a production company, and he told me he would like to film the teaser! I was over the moon, and was so grateful that this happening for me. John was in his last year of university and arranged for me to hold the castings in an office at his Uni. I called up the shortlisted actors on the Starnow website based on their look, and asked them to come down and audition. A range of different experiences came through the door and I met some wonderful people. After three days of casting, I had trouble deciding who the characters were going to be for the teaser.

It was March 2011, I had done the auditions and now what I needed was a location for filming. Simone was kind enough to allow me to use her flat for one of the locations, but I was lacking a house for the main location. I sent a text to everyone in my phone asking who could lend me their dining area for a day. I had a few replies, I looked over a few houses and one of them was great. There was one house that did appeal to me; I went there to have a look. The owner of the house was a friend of a friend and he asked me what my show was about. After telling him, he told me his wife was in another country for two weeks and I could use the whole of his house to film. Not just the teaser but the whole episode! Amazing! I now had a location, film crew and possible actors. The next step was to hold a workshop for the actors so I could select who was going to get the role. The actor (Jason Pennycooke) who plays 'Granddad' in 'All About The McKenzies', originally applied for the role of the dad 'Raymond McKenzie'. Visually, he didn't suit what I had in mind. How it came about for him to play Granddad was that in his photos on his acting CV, I saw a photo of him looking like a granddad. I questioned him about it and he told me it was for a role he played on stage. This gave me an idea, as to date I had no granddad actors. I told him to prepare for an audition for granddad and he arrived dressed as one blowing me away in the audition. It was at that moment I knew he 'was' Granddad.

I used the owner's house for the workshops and what a great and exciting day it was. I felt so happy I was doing something I love by acting on an idea and taking the action necessary to see it's fulfilment. A few days later, I was going through the camcorder looking over the workshop that was filmed. I had a clipboard out and noted down all the actors who took part. I was taking notes but I found it so difficult to choose who was going to get the role. I called up Simone and she came around my house and we viewed the footage together. After a huge debate, we finally decided who the selected actors were, so now it was time to tell the actors. All I needed now was a director. There was one lady who was interested and she met with Simone and I for a meeting. She had drawn up a storyboard for the opening scene, which was very exciting to see. Everything was all good. She told me about what she did other than directing, and her main job was working as an air hostess. My only concern was her availability for rehearsals and filming, which when stated she said it would have been fine.

Rehearsals were needed before the filming so we could make things easier on the day if actors knew exactly what to do. Actors were asked to bring different clothes from their wardrobe so we could see what the options were. Prior to the rehearsal date I was on the phone to the actress who was going to play Charlene McKenzie. I had a conversation with her and I caught a vibe that she was telling me how to run my production. Immediately, flags went up in my head as I couldn't have that attitude when filming. After I got off the phone with her, I had to think of a plan B and have a security replacement. I gave her the benefit of the doubt by allowing her to attend rehearsals, but I also had another actress attend rehearsals for the role of Charlene. On the day of the rehearsal, the original actress to play Charlene walked out! She was angry by the fact I had another girl there as *'security'.* She didn't want the role and told me to give it to the other girl. My response was very positive as I refused to let this show go down the drain. The other actress ended up getting the role instead. Another challenge on the day of rehearsals was that the director never turned up! I couldn't get through to her phone and she wasn't responding to me, not just on this day but for a whole week! When I did hear back from the director, I immediately told her I did not want her to be part of the production anymore, as she had put me on the spot by not showing up or being accessible. Her excuse was she was working, but hadn't we had a meeting to confirm availabilities? If she had told me she was unavailable, then I wouldn't have given her the job. After talking with Carolyn, she told me about some projects she did at university which she had directed. As I was desperate, and I had no replacement director, I allowed her to do her thing so I made her director of the show.

A lot of twists and turns, you're thinking? You haven't even heard half of it! I had a phone call from Carolyn out of the blue three days before filming and she informed me we had no equipment! I was perplexed because I thought it was all sorted. No. The person who was looking after all the filming equipment had gone away on holiday and there was no access to the equipment for a few more weeks, which meant the 'so-called' production company was not happening anymore. I was devastated. I'm not going to lie, readers, I was disappointed because Carolyn told me she had it all sorted and I trusted her with the role given to her seeing as I was occupied with so many other areas. I told her to sort something out as I had other things to be looking into. By being the person in charge of your own production, you are responsible for the outcome of the whole show. Even though Carolyn was responsible for the crew, I had to step in and do an emergency advertisement online at mandy.com for a cameraman and sound recorder. This required money, so I had to speak to my parents and conduct a Dragon's Den with them to ask for money to advertise and pay the crew. They happily invested, so I found a solution to the problem within the same day. That evening I called Carolyn and asked her if there had been any development from her end in terms of sorting things out. She replied that there was still no equipment. At this point, I told her that I had already sorted it and found a completely different crew to film the pilot. The truth was she didn't even know what to do and hadn't even looked to find a solution; she left it all to me to sort out!

The first day of filming was April 22nd. Remember when I said I wrote down a goal stating that I will be in production by April 21st? Well, it came true! Carolyn was late and a couple of members of the crew didn't like the way she conducted herself and neither did I. It was like she was making all the decisions without confronting me first - *she forgot who the producer was*. I also noticed on the call sheets that she had written up, she called herself the executive producer! Simone had called me to find out what was going on as she had received emails from Carolyn giving her demands about what to do on the production, which left Simone feeling out of place. I thought I would leave it and sort it out after the day of filming just so we could at least get on with the day with no bad vibes. I sent Carolyn an email the night before the next filming date telling her the members of crew didn't like the way she came across. I put in my personal views in a professional manner and she replied saying she didn't want to be a part of the production anymore knowing that people were thinking of her in that way. She quit on the day of filming, which was a lot of pressure for me as I now had to step in as director. I hadn't had any directing experience before and didn't really know what I was doing, but we ended up getting the day of filming done.

The pilot was only three days of filming and there was one day where the cameraman turned up very late telling me the sound recorder was sick, so wasn't attending. I was under a lot of pressure as there was a lot to film and there was no crew. After two hours, the cameraman turned up and had the cheek to tell me to me he had to leave filming early as he had some event to go to in the evening. There was no apology whatsoever! I had to bite my tongue as I just wanted to get the day done. I felt the filming had been rushed since the cameraman had to leave early. Needless to say, I wasn't satisfied at all. I felt bad having to ask the cast members to come out another day so we could reshoot everything as I wanted quality, not something that was rushed! The cameraman agreed to come out again but I had to pay him more money! luckily, I was able to have the sound recorder this time! Apart from that I was grateful for the cast to come out of their way to do the reshoot as it wasn't their fault. With everything completed I thanked the crew and cast, and told the crew I would collect the rushes from them during the week. Little did I know this decision was the biggest mistake.

Phone calls, emails, texts, and voice messages had been ignored for weeks! I was calling up the cameraman so I could collect the rushes from the whole shoot and there was no response. I didn't understand it. Lots of thoughts were racing through my mind about what to do. I even looked up his office address and drove round there and was banging on the door, but there was no response. Where had this guy gone? I called up the sound guy, but he didn't understand it either, so I asked him for the cameraman's address, but he wouldn't give it to me as it was confidential. I explained to him how urgent this was. I needed the material, as I couldn't go forward without it. He assured me he would contact the cameraman himself. I wouldn't say I was patient in this matter as you could probably understand. He eventually sent me a text one morning saying he was busy and couldn't respond to my messages. *Can you believe that?! You're telling me after three weeks you didn't have ten seconds to tell me that you were busy?!* He told me to go to his office and collect my stuff. When I went round there, I had one thing in mind, *get the rushes, don't make conversation and get out!* I had had enough of this guy - he was so unprofessional!

After I had transferred the rushes onto the hard-drive, I was so relieved and happy that I could finally move onto the next stage and never have to deal with that guy again! Excited as I was, I remember returning home to view some of the rushes on my laptop and I felt a massive pain in my chest when I had discovered IT WASN'T THE WHOLE EPISODE!!! There was footage missing from another camera. I had to contact the cameraman again to find out where all my rushes were and surprise, surprise the same thing happened... SILENCE AND IGNORANCE!!! I called the sound guy back straight away and told him everything; he told me he was having trouble getting in touch with him too, and the cameraman's attitude toward him had changed. He said he would keep on contacting him for me. I told him he should go on the computer himself, and grab the rushes, but he said he couldn't do that as after all they were business partners, thus he didn't want to get on the wrong side of his partner. I had to put him in his place and reiterate that this project meant so much to me and my life was literally on hold until I got that footage. He said there was nothing he could do. All I had was rushes of the first scene in the pilot. I contacted a friend who edited a show I worked on for BBC called *'The Cut'* and asked if he could edit what I had. Thankfully, he agreed and we ended up with a three-minute scene for the beginning of the episode. It was great to watch, but at the back of my mind I was still disappointed that it wasn't the whole episode. Further to the madness, Simone called me to say she had to leave the production due to her finding another job. I couldn't believe this whole production was crumbling down and people were leaving etc. *Was there anyone who believed in me to stick for the full run?* After many attempts of communication to the camera guy and no response, I felt lost and defeated and didn't know what to do.

During these times of hardship, I landed an acting role on Eastenders E20, which lifted my spirits. It was a month of filming throughout May 2011. So much was learnt on set, and my attitude was of a producer. I was asking questions from crew members, shadowing the director and picking the brains of the producer. I also used my initiative to investigate the ins and outs of the main Eastenders production. I wanted to know who the directors were, and most of all, the decision makers. At the cast and crew party, I got talking with one of the directors, 'Lee Salisbury', we got on very well and suggested I pop into his office on some downtime during the filming so we could continue our chat. Without wasting time, the next day I walked into his office and told him what happened to my show. I asked him if after the filming of E20 he would allow me to shadow him on set and watch his every move. He didn't mind and told me he would need to speak to the series producer. Originally, the series producer had said *"no"* when I had asked, but when Lee asked then the decision was a *"yes".* I was now on the set of Eastenders, shadow directing and I guess you could call me a sponge as I soaked up a lot about production and directing.

From that experience, I felt more elevated after my defeat with the McKenzies pilot. I felt motivated to use the knowledge I had learnt. It was as if the *'directing'* and *'writing'* talent was unlocked within me. I received a Facebook message from a guy called Israr, who had just finished university and was looking for work. I met with him in Starbucks in Tottenham Court road to explain an idea I had about filming actors demo reels for them. I was to write and direct the scenes and he was to be the cameraman and editor. After buying some cheap sound equipment (microphone and boom pole) I had contacted a few friends on Facebook and told them what I was doing and used them as guinea pigs, so I had examples to show people of what I could do. This would result in a service providing actors who have no demo reel the chance to have something visual which they could put on their online acting CVs. I received a few phone calls and we got some work out of it. This was adding further experience to my writing and directing. I also learned a lot from Israr.

SEVEN AND A HALF MONTHS SINCE THE MCKENZIES DISASTER. My phone rang. My friend Pauline just got back from Philadelphia from a Tasha Smith acting workshop. She was blown away and told me there was going to be the Hollywood Black Film Festival happening in October 2011, so she suggested I go out there as she thought it would do me good and you never know who I'd meet. I had some money aside so I thought, why not? After all, I literally didn't know what else to do with my show. I flew out there by myself and stayed with a friend. The Hollywood Black Film Festival (HBFF) was only for a few days consisting of panels, screenings of films, and a monologue slam, which I took part in with the casting director 'Twinkie Bird'. One panel, in particular, had a guest speaker called Michael Ajakwe, who had written for a lot of black sitcoms in the states such as: 'Martin', 'Moesha', 'The Parkers' just to name a few, and was the co-producer for 'Sister Sister' and 'Eve'.

During the Q&A, I shared a brief description of my experience with the Mckenzies. The room went silent. After the panel had finished, Michael approached me, took my hand, and gave me his card, he said, *"don't let anyone know I gave you that"*. He also told me he was the founder of the Los Angeles Web Festival and told me there was another festival coming up in April 2012 (5 months away). He said that I needed to get my show submitted for it. All I could think was *"OMG are you saying I need to go through that whole process again and film from scratch?!"*. We exchanged details and I went back to my friend's house.

(Pics from HBFF 2011)

By being in LA, I was introduced to the idea of 'Web-series'. I never really knew what they were until I went there. It is very popular out there and I felt like the UK was so far behind, because I didn't know anyone who had a web-series. As I was packing my suitcase to return home to London, thoughts were haunting me about how I was going to have to re-film everything! Just then I received a text message. IT WAS THE SOUND GUY FROM THE MCKENZIES PILOT FROM SEVEN AND HALF MONTHS AGO! He said he was in Italy and that he managed to retrieve all my footage from the cameraman. He announced that he was no longer in business with that guy anymore as he found out he was ripping people off by taking their money and not returning the goods! He said he would post me a USB with everything on it as the files were huge! You can imagine how I felt at this moment... I was over the moon! So much waiting around and I thought I would never see my footage again, not only that, I didn't have to film anything else as it was already filmed, it only needed editing.

(Myself and Spencer Collins) *(Myself and Kym Whitley)*

My friend who I was staying with was friends with an actress in Los Angeles, and said she would introduce me. I didn't know who she was talking about, she told me her name but I didn't know who the actress was until I checked her out on IMDB... The actress was 'Karen Malina White'.

(Karen Malina White and me)

Karen had starred in shows that I grew up on! Such as *'Malcom and Eddie', 'The Cosby Show', 'Hangin' with Mr Cooper', 'A Different World', 'The Bernie Mac Show',* she did the voice for the character 'Dijonay' in *'The Proud Family'* and she was also Jazz's girlfriend in *'The Fresh Prince of Bel Air'*. I felt honoured to be in the presence of this woman having admired her during my childhood, as she used to make me laugh all the time! We hung out and she shared her knowledge of the industry, talking to me about certain stars she knew. I think I was more hung up with the fact that this woman worked with Will Smith! I forgot to mention, whilst I was in LA, I met some people who attended the festival who seemed like potential friends I would have for a long time, so we kept each other's details as you never know what could happen in the future. I left for London the next day with a big smile on my face.

Back in London and after about four weeks I received the USB. I took it back to the editor leaving him to deal with it. I was giddy and acting like a kid! I told him the requirements of the festival stated that any submission that was comedy had to be under seven minutes long, and if he could chop up the episode and make three seven minutes long. Little did I know, I would receive a phone call back within a few hours with some very upsetting news. The editor told me that everything that was filmed consisted of a lot of dodgy camera work. Shots were out of focus, and there was no way any of what was filmed originally could have been used! He said it would be unprofessional to submit what was filmed as it would make me look bad. There were now two options in my mind, quit or start again.

CHAPTER 3

READY, SET, GO! SERIES 1

Ask yourselves this, what would you have done after all of that? I refused to give up, plus I felt I had gained a lot more knowledge based on my experience. It was January 2012. I knew I had two months to submit something to the festival. March 6th was the deadline. A friend at the time had introduced me to a music producer as I wanted to get back on with my music. I had a meeting with this guy and we sat down and discussed a few things. He asked me more about what else I had done and I told him the embarrassing story of the McKenzie's pilot. I showed him the three-minute clip I had on a private link online and discussed the festival with him. He then told me to that his mum worked for a sound company and would be able to get some sound equipment, and we should get to work on getting the web-series done if I paid him £250. This gave me hope that I was going to make the deadline. After putting all my cards on the table, I knew I had to find out from the cast if they were going to be available. Also with that thought, I knew I wanted to change the actress who played Charlene McKenzie, as I found the second Charlene quite unprofessional. After calling up the cast, I discovered the actor who played Raymond McKenzie had left the country, because he got married to a woman in Bahrain. He also needed to be replaced, so I contacted another actor 'Sheldon Nichols', who was shortlisted for his part when we originally cast and gave it to him. The actress who played Annika had some family troubles she was going through, so she also needed replacing.

I decided to hold another casting for Charlene and Annika. After a few auditions, I discovered 'Ria Horsford', who was then offered the role of Charlene McKenzie as I found her magnificent, plus I remember watching her perform in a play in August 2011. Now that I found my cast and knew everyone's time frames, I needed to re-write certain parts of my original script. However, because of timing, what I did was look at my original scripts and select chunks from it and change aspects of it to suit a web episode that was under seven minutes long. I had timed in my head the duration whilst reading the final script and it seemed to me that everything was under seven minutes. I forwarded the scripts to the cast and was on a mission to look for filming locations.

I wasn't allowed to use the original house as the owner had moved to another country, so I asked my next-door neighbour if we could use his house for the upstairs rooms which would represent the bedrooms for the characters, Samuell, and Andre, and the bathroom. I knew I needed a school, so I spoke to a head teacher whom I knew at Gladesmore Community School in Tottenham. *I was known at this school for helping them with their school project for their anti-gun campaign Value Life in 2010*. The head teacher said this would be fine but I had to be CRB checked and get the parental consent for each student wanting to get involved. I got typing away and created a permission form. The teacher then suggested I promote the opportunity in the school assembly. So, one morning I was allowed five minutes on the stage to present it. I said I needed roughly thirty students to represent a classroom and told them to collect the forms off the head teacher and I would be back the following week to collect them. My long-time friend Sarah allowed me to use her house to film in to represent the house belonging to the character 'Annika'. The actor who played Raymond McKenzie said that he would speak to his mum about letting me use her house for filming in. *This was to be the living room and kitchen area.* I went round there to have a look and it looked perfect for what I had imagined. The mother agreed, so I gave her the dates for when we would be filming.

During these times, I was advertising on my Facebook. The series was on its way to creating hype. I didn't think people knew what I was planning or what it took to plan such a thing. I knew I was going to be the director and producer because I knew I was a lot more confident to execute the task based on the experience I got from Eastenders and directing actors' reels. I went to my parents and explained to them what I was doing and that I needed £250 to pay the sound guy, and eventually they gave me the money. I put my car off the road so I could save a bit more money so cast and crew would be able to be fed on the days of filming. *I just want to note to the reader that during the whole duration since the start of the Mckenzies, I was not working, I was on benefits 'job seekers allowance'. This allowed me the time to get on with the show. I did work for a call centre for a couple of months, but it killed me. As it was not what I wanted to do. I was depressed and my show was all I could think about, so I had to make the sacrifice of leaving the work place to make it happen.*

I was contacted on Facebook by a girl named Marla who wanted to be a production assistant. She wanted to assist in any way she could on the production. I was open to receive any help where possible. I told her about the previous experiences I had from people who wanted to help and she said she would be fully committed, so I took her on. Marla was in charge of contacting all the students' parents and dealing with admin. *You'll later find out that I ended up doing the admin myself.* It was estimated that the series would take five days to film between February 12th 2012 – February 17th 2012. There would be enough time afterwards to get the show edited and there was confidence that I would make the deadline. I learned how to devise a production schedule by looking at a schedule which was given to me on Eastenders E20 *(Marla was supposed to take care if this but she didn't!).* Marla had a day job, I can't remember what it entailed, but she didn't have time to sort out the schedule. Being my first experience, it took me hours to figure out how production companies put these documents together, but *I got there in the end.*

Preparations were made for the weekly shoots. I continued to use Israr as my cameraman and editor as I had formed a solid working relationship with him with past projects since the pilot disaster. I made sure I had an external hard drive to transfer all rushes and sound files from the day onto it. *I learned my lesson from last time for not having one.* On the first day of filming Marla never turned up. She had the excuse that she was *"too tired"* to come in as she had a family function the night before. I was furious, obviously. The day was snowy and certain cast members were having trouble getting to the location. As this was now eating into filming time, I had to arrange for a car to pick them up from the station. The sound guy had two assistants with him to help him out; I thought this was very handy as it would make things speed up quicker. It even helped when the sound guy had an extra camera that we could use to help speed up the filming process. I was happy that after the last disaster things were starting to pan out for me.

OBSTACLES

I want the reader to know during this process I felt major resistance in my mind as I was learning and was going along. I didn't have the know-how for the whole process and I literally had to deal with obstacles as and when they came. On the first filming day, we didn't finish every scene. I had to make sure that those scenes were completed on the next day we were due to be back at this location. My experience from E20 and other productions taught me that the challenge was getting everything filmed within a certain time-frame, and if scenes were taking long, *'quality'* had to be cut down from the scene i.e. *the way it is shot*. For series 1, we had no makeup or costume department, cast did their own makeup and wore their own wardrobe. There was no lighting; we literally shot with the light that was available to us at the time. After all, the only people that got paid were the sound guy and Israr, cast and locations did this for free! I think it says a lot about cast members when they can come out of their way for free, giving up their time to perform for something they believe in. They saw what I was trying to do and I had so much love for them. Another obstacle I had to overcome with this series was when sound files accidentally got deleted during a scene and we had to film those scenes again. This required more time for cast and crew to stay behind which created frustration on set. Jason Pennycooke (Granddad) had his daughter on set one day and the night before he rung me up asking if I could prioritize his scenes as he didn't want his daughter hanging around. This was understandable, so one night after filming I had to rejig the schedule and make it possible.

Dealing with school students can be a challenge especially when you are dealing with thirty of them and you are trying to run a show. The students had no idea what being an extra was about. Yes, they knew it involved being in the background but they didn't know the reality of being an extra having to wait around for long periods of time. They were getting restless and so was the head teacher. During filming at the school, we had so much fun but the obstacle was when the teacher told me at the last minute that we had to be out of the school earlier than expected. This was due to school caretakers etc., but *I don't really remember what the actual reason was.* An assistant who I met on Eastenders E20, volunteered to help out with recording when I contacted him, as the main sound guy had to leave at a certain time. He was taught how to use the equipment fast and he was good to go. I would say that during this day at the school, I received a negative impression from the sound crew because at one point during filming we were ready to shoot and the sound crew were nowhere to be found. It turned out that since their equipment was downstairs and we were filming upstairs they thought I would not notice their absence. They were going off to the shops during filming to get themselves some food. I lost respect for them after that, but I had to keep my cool as I wanted the day complete.

There was one dramatic day on the last day of filming where one of the sound guy's assistants got stabbed in the face at a petrol station. I was shocked! And didn't know how to respond when I was told. Even though this had happened the assistant who got stabbed still chose to come in during that day of filming and help out. I told him that I would understand if he didn't want to come out, but he was determined and said he had seen what *I have had to go through getting the show done and that he couldn't let me down.* I was grateful and we completed the day. Out of the series, one scene had to be cancelled due to lack of time *which is why when you watch the series you'll notice episode five is only three and a half minutes long.*

With everything filmed and *'in the can'* as they would say in the film world, it was fair to say that congratulations were in order! It had been an intense five-day shoot with various temperatures and different types of weather, snow, rain, and sun *but hey, that's British weather for you!* Now all that was needed was for the edit and getting the music composed. During the days of directing actors' reels, my old friend from high school *'Zabdiel'*, and I bumped into each other on the high street one day, and he had told me he was studying music composition for film. I told him about the show and he was all for composing for it. I told him the feel of the show but knowing him, he would automatically connect with the media and know exactly what to compose.

With everything in the process of being edited, I was deciding how the trailer was going to look. I needed something that would get people's attention and create hype. As the show is narrated I thought to narrate the trailer as well. Once I had the narration figured out, I went to the studio to record my vocal. It was with this vocal that I started to figure out images that were filmed in the show that would work around it. It was the first ever series so I had to introduce the characters in a stylistic way which would make an audience want to know the characters. In forming the idea, Israr called me with some bad news, but even before he spoke a flashback of my past experiences flashed before me and was dreading what he had to tell me. It turned out that there were a lot of issues with the sound files, everything from distortion to low volume, and all other kinds of problems. I told him to send me the rough cut of the first episode and I was very disappointed in the quality of the sound. At this moment, I actually thought I was cursed. The equipment the sound guys had looked so professional, so I didn't understand why the quality was so low! I even paid £250 for this! I then found out that the main sound guy who got the equipment in the first place had no knowledge on the subject whatsoever! He didn't know how to mix sound all he did on the days of filming was press record. *This will answer some of your questions as to why series one sound quality wasn't the best!*

I wanted the best! I wanted something to look and sound 'wow!' It was embarrassing on my behalf to come out with a series that sounded not on point. Some of you may notice that it may sound all right, but *that's understandable for people who are not attuned to the technicalities.* If I were to play the series on bigger speakers, everyone would notice that there are sound problems. Online you may notice it a little bit, but it's enough for you to get away with. There wasn't much I could do about it as the festival date was just around the corner and I needed something to submit. After the series had been edited roughly, Israr sent me the video files and I made notes as to what changes to make etc. and then he would amend where necessary. Once I was satisfied with the final cut I would then forward it to Zab and he would compose music to it. The moment I had the final masters of the files I immediately sent out the clips to the festival and played the waiting game. After about a week I was contacted by Michael Ajakwe and told that All About The McKenzies was selected to be screened at the LA Web Festival 2012! Proud? You bet I was. I was going to be flying back out to LA and have my show screened with an American audience! I told the cast members and they were happy. I booked my flight and within two weeks I was flying out to LA!

LOS ANGELES WEB FESTIVAL 2012

The web festival was being held at the Radisson Hotel near LAX airport. I was staying in the hotel as my friend from last year wasn't available. I had flyers printed for my show to give out to anyone who was interested in watching the series. The hotel was beautiful and it felt great to be back in LA! After a nice hot shower, I thought it was best to reflect on the whole journey up to that point, and what a journey it was! Remembering the moment I was with my friend brainstorming ideas for the show, remembering when I quit my call centre job to make a commitment to myself that why would I waste my life force working for somebody else who didn't care about me, but about themselves making money, remembering the disaster of losing all my rushes for the pilot, having it retrieved and then told I couldn't use it, remembering the Hollywood Black Film Festival and knowing that that moment led up to where I was in this very hotel room. The view from my room was amazing, I could see the Hollywood sign and staring out the window gave me a feeling of '*wow this is where I want to be - this is why I'm doing what I'm doing*'!

On the day of the festival I was asked by one of the staff members if I would be interested in speaking on one of the panels. I was flattered, and so agreed. The panel was all about creating a webseries from scratch, and boy, did I have a story. I had the opportunity to meet various webseries' creators. One in particular was a guy called Timothy who was from France; he wanted to interview me and put a link to my series on his website in France. Of course, I wasn't going to say no, that means there would be more promotion for the McKenzies! I looked at the schedule for the screenings and it was nice to see my show in the LA Web Festival magazine! There were series of all genres and it was inspiring. What was also empowering to know was that I was the *only* young black individual from London UK that attended the festival!

It was time for the screenings and I sat in the room watching different content with many hopefuls that wanted to showcase their talent and worth in the industry. The internet has proven to provide an abundance of opportunities for everyone, everyone has a story, not just I, but everyone and we choose to express it through doing a series, whatever the purpose or intention may be. Some series I enjoyed, some I thought were too long, some were too short, and as I viewed each person's content I was relating to each piece as it taught me a valuable lesson about doing a next series. You could also tell people's experience levels from the difference in quality. Remember Karen Malina White? I invited her to my screening and she attended! When "All About The McKenzies" started, I cringed because I didn't know what response I was going to get, plus I was conscious of the fact that my sound quality wasn't the best. I got a few laughs and was happy about the response. There were a few people that made a comment regarding the sound quality, but I explained the situation, and they understood. One creator told me that they made sure they invested in a decent sound guy as the sound is so important because if we are struggling to hear something, we will switch off. Even if the image quality isn't perfect, at least if the sound is good we can still pay attention. This was so true when I heard this because I have experienced it before with certain videos on Youtube where the image wasn't great but I could hear what was going on. Karen enjoyed the show, congratulated me, and left.

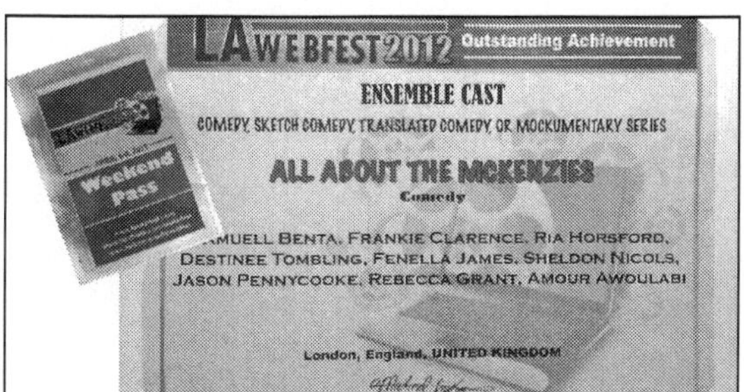

(pic of certificate)

The next evening was the award ceremony and I contacted someone I had met from the Hollywood Black Film Festival from the previous year whose name was Tyra. She was able to attend the award ceremony for the festival and support me. I was hoping that my show was going to win some sort of award as it would have been such an achievement, *especially the fact that it was in LA!* It was a great night supported with a live jazz/funk band and the hall was packed! Everyone who created a series was there, and Michael was the host of the evening. *This may sound cheesy but I felt like I was at the Oscars!* After about an hour, it finally got to discussing the genre of Comedy. I remember sitting there thinking I must win something, I've put so much into this show. Hearing everyone else's show being called out for particular categories and not mine made me feel a bit disappointed but, lo and behold All About The Mckenzies won an award for "Great Ensemble Cast in a Comedy".

All About the McKenzies

With Samuell Benta

(Indie Source Magazine Summer2012)

Worth it? You bet it was! There were more interviews conducted and other magazines wanting to talk to me for publication in their next issue.

Now all that was left was for the UK to know about the show. After flying back home I said that May 1st 2012 would be the premiere of the first episode. The date at the time was April 12th 2012, so I had to let as many people know about the show as possible. I promoted the show on Facebook, Twitter, YouTube, I even had people I met from the festival promoting it for me from different countries on their websites: Germany, France, USA etc. There were a couple of radio stations who reached out to me once they saw the trailer posted online to interview me. Episode 1 aired and *boy did I get a response. I had so much attention for a 4-minute clip - it was unbelievable.* Everyone was hungry for more. The 4-minute episode was teasing them and they were frustrated by the length of it. In fact, *most people* made comments saying that the episode was too short and that the show deserved to be longer. *Little did they know that originally the show was meant to be longer.*

During the hype of the first episode, there was a huge buzz where I had to start getting my 'producer hat' on, as certain individuals and companies wanted to know who I was. There was one company in particular who specialised in urban content online *(I won't mention their name for legal reasons).* They spoke to me on the phone and wanted to know more about my show, and they spoke to me about growing my audience. This was attractive as I wanted as many people to know about the show as possible, but I didn't know that there would be consequences. They wanted a meeting with me as soon as possible and they asked me not to post anymore episodes online until we had that meeting! I then told them that the meeting had to be within the week because I was planning to release the second episode. In the meeting, there were deep discussions about what this company could do for me etc. and this was the first proper meeting I ever had of this nature. The company was offering me their platform to grow my audience and awareness. I was allowed to keep all creative control and they would offer me the equipment I needed to make a second series possible. What they wanted out of it was for my show to be uploaded to their YouTube channel, but they wanted my YouTube channel shutdown, and they wanted 40% of the rights to my show. I was still trying to digest all of this considering what I had been through as this information was virgin to my mind. They said they would draw up a contract and that they will leave me time to think. Because I was in two minds about what to do, I had to hold off posting more episodes of the Mckenzies. If this deal was to follow through, I needed legal advice.

There was one TV channel, OHTV, that wanted the McKenzies on their channel with 30-minute episodes. I had a meeting with them and they saw the video I edited together from what I had experienced at the LA Web festival with the Americans' response. We also watched a few more episodes of the first series (not yet released online). As flattered as I was, I didn't think that the show was right for their channel judging by what they currently broadcast. With all this attention, I didn't know what to do as I didn't have the "*know-how*" or knowledge of how this side of the industry worked. I purchased a book about producing new media just to get some data as to how this all worked.

One day I got a tweet from Frankie Clarence who plays 'Andre Mckenzie' and he told me about an event that was taking place at the BFI in Southbank. I attended with flyers for the McKenzies in my bag. It was an event to do with Black Filmmakers in the UK, and there was a panel of people who were doing a talk about the subject of black filmmakers raising finance. I was shocked to see that one person on the panel was *'Tim Reid'* who played the dad in *'Sister Sister',* he had some insightful knowledge to share with the audience. I made sure I had my notepad and pen to take notes. After the event, I introduced myself to everyone on the panel *and I got to talk to Tim!* Another exciting giddy moment, but I wasn't there for jokes. This was serious - I needed information. One lady in particular was on her way out, but I managed to catch up with her. She went by the name of Mary and I gave her my flyer for the show and she gave me her card. The event went well and I promoted my show to everybody by giving out flyers.

The next day I emailed everybody with whom I had networked and I had a response from Mary. I spoke to her in more detail about my show and the attention I was getting etc. She requested that she watch the whole series. After careful consideration, I sent her the whole series on private links for her to view. It wasn't even a day before I got a response and Mary wanted to help me with my journey with the show. She knew an entertainment lawyer who could help me figure out what the deal was between the urban media company. She sorted me out a meeting with him. To cut a long story short, the lawyer looked over the contract and told me that I wasn't getting anything from this company which I hadn't already done myself! Plus, they were asking a lot from me and weren't looking to put any funds toward the show, which didn't make sense! *I just want the reader to note that at this point the Mckenzies was on hold online; no more episodes had been released for three weeks since the first until I had an answer regarding this contract. To let viewers know what was going on, I had to post a video stating that the show was on hold for important reasons.*

The decision was made and I turned the urban media company down and released the second episode. The problem I had at the time was getting the buzz back on the show. Due to the three-week gap, the momentum had been lost. In the meantime, Mary said to me that her 8-year-old daughter loved the show and it got me thinking, because I had a bit of contact with mothers telling me their kids loved the show and they were all under the age of 10. I was starting to think maybe going down the under 10yr old route for the show. After all, I treated this first series as a test to see audience response in order to navigate where it was going and who it would cater to. A few more weeks went by and 99.9% of people loved the show. I remained a fly on the wall monitoring who was watching and where they watched it from. It turned out that my core audience were people aged between 13 – 26. I decided to reach out to various different TV networks that catered towards children's content, under 13s primarily, because of the response I got from mothers! I was surprised to get a response back from CBBC within a day! They had viewed the trailer and first episode and wanted questions answered. In response to their request, I provided the breakdown of the series and characters and told them that the show was in its baby stages where changes could be made. Mary intervened and was kind of like a PA to me as she knew how to deal with emails to big companies such as the BBC etc. She taught me the art of emailing professionally and I noticed it from looking at the way she spoke to professionals, she also taught me 'business talk' noticing the bullshitters from the serious people. I had a lot of respect for Mary.

A meeting was booked and within a month myself and Mary were on a train to Manchester to the CBBC Drama department to meet with a couple of executive producers. Nervous? You bet I was! I was in a suit and prepared to talk about the Mckenzies. Prior to the meeting, I made sure to inform myself of their current productions so I wouldn't attend in ignorance or show lack of interest in their network. Their only concern was that the McKenzies would be too similar to a show they currently have, which was called 'The 4 o'clock club'. I had made it very clear that my show was completely different. We watched a couple more episodes on my laptop and it was nice to see middle-aged white women laughing at the show. There was a comment regarding the show being too obviously similar in terms of race to one of their productions. They weren't straight to the point about what they meant but I came and said it *"is it because they are all black?"* in which they replied "yes". They wanted further information but the meeting came to an end, and it resulted in them saying that they would love to work with me on another project.

I was very emotional after the meeting because I was certain at that point my show was going to be taken to the next level. Mary had to reassure me that I took a huge step in having a meeting in the first place. It takes some people years to get a meeting and I got one within a month of contacting them, which made me feel a bit better. Mary said that the lead was not dead because they left the connection open for me in terms of another project; she said I needed to get my head screwed on and think about how I can still move with the McKenzies, but at the same time creatively combine it with another show that catered more towards their market.

Back in London, I was a prisoner in my bedroom figuring out how to create something from the McKenzies for CBBC. After endless coffees and hours of no food, ignoring my mobile phone calls, I slapped myself for stupidity as the answer was staring me at my face all the time… by staring at the family promo picture one character stood out to me… ANGEL MCKENZIE! How old was Angel? 10 years old! Perfect! There will be a spinoff show from the McKenzies called 'ANGEL MCKENZIE' the life through *'her'* eyes. The eyes of a 10-year-old girl who a lot of kids could relate to! My brain cells were bubbling and ideas flew to my consciousness. This show was going to be a hit like *'Hannah Montana'* and all those huge American shows that girls love! I won't get into too much detail regarding ANGEL MCKENZIE, but let's just say that I devised a treatment and full character description that CBBC loved! The final decision would be based on what their controller had to say, but all in all it was an amazing idea that hit their criteria. This is what their email had said:

Dear Samuel!

As promised we've finally managed to get together to discuss your ideas for *Angel McKenzie*. Sorry it's a bit later than perhaps we'd hoped but we hope you find our thoughts useful because Angel McKenzie is a terrific character: she's warm and funny and manages to bring a good sense of normality to an otherwise exceptional world. Her multiple talents mean that she could be quite a remote or aloof character for our audience and yet her clear humanity -- the ordinariness of her trials and tribulations -- means she's clearly someone our audience could easily engage with. And that's quite a feat -- creating a character who's both brilliant AND likeable/easy to identify with takes real talent and it's done with great aplomb here

(The Angel McKenzie logo.. All Rights Reserved)

It was another waiting game to get a response from them about their controller's decision, and I was very positive. During these times, all episodes were now online and people wanted more. I had to smile because it was great that people loved something that I wrote and slaved away at for ages! I also thought to myself that people really do not know what it takes to create a show and get it to a stage of even putting it online for them to watch for free. I had a meeting with Mary and she was excited about 'ANGEL MCKENZIE', but now she spoke to me on a more serious level which I would say is where I had a growth spurt mentally. Now that the series was online for everyone to get a taste of what the show is all about. The decision had to be made about the direction of it, i.e.:

- Who is it for?
- Do we still keep knocking on TV Network's doors?

- Do we go independent etc.?

Silence was mainly my answer for the whole meeting, as I was nearly in tears because this whole journey was *'unexpected'*. When I originally started, a webseries was not even on my radar because I didn't know that they existed. Not only that, everything since I started came as and when, nothing was planned. I didn't know how things would pan out or that it would even be this way in the first place! I called it walking in faith and not by sight. I just wanted to ACT! *This is the thing readers, you've already read about the process so far, I'm sure you can agree with me when I say that I didn't know how things would pan out.*

One evening I went to an event which took place in Waterloo, as I knew there was going to be a lady from Channel 4 doing a presentation about 'Diversity in TV programming'. This appealed to me because clearly the issue was that there was hardly anything diverse on British screens except for predominantly white faces. I knew with my show I could make a change but up to this point I had been running for miles and nothing concrete except a webseries that was online. The lady *(I'll call her Carol for the sake of this book and legal reasons),* presented an eye-opening presentation and it seemed like what she presented. I had an answer for her... my show! I managed to speak to her after the presentation about my show and gave her a flyer. She said she would check it out. Quicker than I expected, I got an email the next day saying she had watched it during her lunch break and was hooked! I was happy and I asked her for a meeting so I could explain in detail about the show possibly going to channel 4. She did talk about show diversity after all, and I thought channel 4 would be a great place for the McKenzies.

Mary was very supportive when I shared her info about Channel 4 and my progress. Getting the meeting was taking ages to finalize as there were always cancellations and rescheduling. Emails were sent back and forth and the last thing I wanted was for this to go *cold* which was why I took immediate action. After about a month a meeting was scheduled and I was on my way to Channel 4 to meet with Carol and her manager Sheila. We sat down and I explained to them about the McKenzies. *I was a lot more experienced as I had had a few meetings prior to this.* I said to her that I had 8 episodes ready to go for TV. Sheila was explaining a show that was about to go in production called *'Youngers',* which apparently had been in development for two years and now they were going into production. The meeting lasted roughly 30mins and Sheila asked me to forward her the pilot episode script and a treatment. She said she would be in contact within a month, but she never did.

Frustrated as I was from no response, I was getting rejection emails from other TV networks and thought to myself that this just wasn't going to happen for TV. I'm not a negative thinker, but after the constant push with the show and constant rejections, I really did not know what to do. The only hope I had was the 'Angel McKenzie' project with CBBC, I hadn't received a response at that time, so I thought to send a reminder email *as I know myself that the executives are very busy.* A couple of days later I jumped when I saw a response and I was heavily contemplating whether to open the email. I was filled with excitement and thought it would be wonderful if I was in production for Angel McKenzie and had All About

The McKenzies running parallel to it! To my shock and horror, I read the email and physically felt sick, this was their response:

Dear Samuel!

Apologies it's taken us a while to get back to you about ANGEL MCKENZIE. Cheryl and I have been working through the backlog of proposals – an ongoing process – and I needed to be sure I had clarity before responding to your email.

I'm afraid, after all that, it's not good news. We were impressed with your willingness to adapt your original concept ALL ABOUT THE MCKENZIES into something more appropriate for our audience, but unfortunately ANGEL MCKENZIE just isn't quite distinctive enough for us. There are very few opportunities for new drama titles to break through, given the success of our current slate and desire to recommission our most popular brands. And as we mentioned before, we do already have a lot of performance based shows on the channel (Alesha's Street Dance Stars, The Big Performance, Sadie J, School for Stars, to mention just a few) so ANGEL MCKENZIE just doesn't stand out from the crowd. So I'm very sorry to say we're going to pass on this occasion.

We wish you every luck and hope this does not prevent you from submitting other ideas in the future.

Best wishes

When I say I physically felt sick I meant it! Confusion, shock, and disappointment were the best words to describe this experience. I did so much, invested so much time into readapting and creating something from scratch to *please somebody else, I might add*. Everything was so positive and the executives loved the idea at the time, yes, the Angel McKenzie show may have had a performance streak within it but there was so much more to it. There was fantasy, comedy and more importantly, education. The shows they listed in their email didn't even come close to my vision of ANGEL MCKENZIE. It showed me a lot about the industry, it showed me that although some people may love your idea, it is always down to *'someone else'* to give it the *"OK"*. I was sick of it because *I* believed in the project, *I* believed it could happen and I knew it would be a great success. It then dawned on me... *was it because I have no previous production credits as a producer "professionally" why this decision was made? Or was it because someone else does not have "my vision" or cannot "see it"?* Whatever the questions were, I did not care anymore.

Mary was disappointed as she too was certain CBBC would shine a green light on the project. Arrows were starting to point at the independent route, and with the way I was feeling, I felt like I needed to be the boss where no one could tell me what can and doesn't work with my show. The decision was made that I would put 'Angel McKenzie' in my archive of things 'to be done' in the near future, but what I currently had with 'All About The McKenzies' was still there. Mary wanted a meeting. Our regular spot was at the BFI in the canteen, and she wanted to talk business. She asked me how could we capitalize on a webseries? I wasn't sure, so I thought it be wise to contact some successful webseries creators in the states to ask them how they profited. I had no response after numerous attempts at reaching out and eventually came to the conclusion that people did not want to share the knowledge. Mary and I came up with a few ideas which made me dig deep with my whole idea about Bentavision and what it represented, because at this point, I was getting a beating from the industry. I wanted something that would offer opportunities, something that would help out the up and coming, something that would be beneficial to the community.

Mary had a word with some investors that she knew and a couple of business partners that she was in business with and arranged a meeting so we could talk about the whole thing. This involved us travelling all the way to Warwickshire, Stratford-upon-Avon, where William Shakespeare was born. We had a meeting in a restaurant and it seemed very promising. At this moment, I thought I was going to get investment to make a second series and knew that I would have some powerful people behind me. They were all older than me and more experienced. The aim of the meeting was really for her business partners to get to know me in order for them to retrieve finance from their investors, as we pretty much had a plan on how we would monetize if we were to do a second series. The substantial amount of views from the first series was a selling point to the investors, so we left the meeting confident that we would get some great feedback. Mary told me that she was going to be travelling for a couple of weeks and would let me know the outcome.

As much as I was gearing towards my dreams and making it happen, I still wasn't making any money as I wasn't working, and it was a stage where I was starting to feel the pinch of the reality. I knew I needed money but at the same time I didn't want to work in a job that I knew would diminish my soul and make me unhappy. *We have all been there and some of you probably are now where you are in a job and there for the sake of 'getting by'*. I refused to have that lifestyle but truth be told, something had to be done, as job-seekers allowance wasn't cutting it for me. I had built up so much trust in Mary over the months as she was helping me along with my journey for which I was so grateful. Because of the relationship that was built with her over time, I felt I could share my concerns about what I could do about my situation that could help. An email was composed and sent airing my personal views. I awaited a response.

One morning I was drinking coffee and making toast in the kitchen thinking to myself about the next possible steps of this journey to where I wanted to go and wanted to achieve, knowing that I had met some great people along the way and *Mary* who taught me a lot, *especially about business acumen.* As per usual I was going through my emails like I do every morning and I received a response from Mary. The email had not acknowledged anything I said to her previously, in fact it completely ignored what I said on a personal level. The response was that she found out from her investors a week ago that they weren't interested in putting up any money towards the project and that she was going to be away for two months in another country on business and wished me good luck with my project. *The point I'm trying to make is, she knew this info "a week ago," and never thought to tell me! Not only that, the tone and manner of her email was "professional" towards me, it wasn't a down to earth friendly email like how we have been communicating over the last few months. Her attitude had changed towards me and it seemed as though because the investors were not interested, "she" wasn't!*

I was knocked out like two legs of my table had been removed. Alone once again, another person walking away and not staying committed. I could be wrong about Mary but it seemed like she gave me a cold brush off because the investors were not interested, and now all of a sudden, she was going to be away for a couple of months. It made me think: *what was her original intention for being involved in the first place? Clearly* it must have been money driven, she did witness networks rejecting me, and she did witness a climax point with CBBC and Channel 4 and it not working out. Who knows what the reason was? All I was looking at was me once again left alone in the wilderness with "All About The Mckenzies". *It was the same feeling I had when I couldn't get hold of the cameraman for the pilot rushes - Crushed!*

So now what? What was I to do? Quit? I had gone too far on this journey to quit now. The date was now September 2012, and looking back at my whole year I was literally *'All about The McKenzies'*. I was the project and the project was me and nothing else, my focus was locked onto it. It can feel very lonely at times when you decide to step out of the box and do something different other than what the masses do by going to work and coming home. No way, I chose to create what I wanted in my life and yes this required sacrifice - nothing ventured nothing gained! I knew that if I could get this show right, everything else that I wanted would come my way and I strongly believed in that! Great news came when I found out that the show was up for nominations for "Best Webseries" for the BEFFTAS (Black Entertainment, Fashion, Film, TV, and Arts awards). The ceremony was going to be in October and all categories were up for public votes. I made sure I posted a video online and asked people to vote if they thought my show deserved it. *I'm one of those people where I'm not going to beg or ask people to do something; I wanted people to vote because they love the show and wanted it to win.*

On the night of the ceremony, two cast members supported me, Frankie, and Fenella. Other cast members were unavailable, unfortunately. The venue was packed and everyone wore their best garments. I was wearing my maroon suit for the first time and call me big-headed but, *I was looking great!* To cut a long story short, after a few hours, it was announced that "All About The McKenzies" won the award for Best Webseries 2012! I and the cast members were on stage and accepted the award. *I would be lying if I were to say that I didn't expect to win, after all this madness with the show, there had to be some reward!*

To check out the first webseries of All about the McKenzies, type in YouTube: All About The Mckenzies series 1, or if you are reading an ebook click here.

CHAPTER 4

HERE WE GROW AGAIN! - SERIES 2

After winning the BEFFTA, I was charged and my belief was stronger this show was meant to be! This was the ultimate creation point where I had analysed all events from idea, to leading up to the moment of the win. I took into account feedback from TV networks, everything I learned with Mary and comments from fans. I told myself that if this was my last chance to make a stand at what I could present to people about myself and my talents, and if there was anyone I admired high up in the industry whom I wanted to see my work, then this was it! I classed the whole journey of this show as a learning curve to mould me into the person I needed to be to do what I was about to do next.

I sat down and looked at all the comments made on all the videos. Most comments were talking about the show being too short, so I decided at that moment that they would be longer. I looked at my analytics and studied who was watching the show and where. I wanted the show to talk to everybody universally, this wasn't just a show online, it was a movement!

In December 2012, whilst looking through my emails one day, there was a message from another urban media company who were very well established. They wanted to know more about my show so we arranged a meeting. *I was a lot more experienced for these meetings and was curious to know what this company had to say*. One thing I loved about the company was their success in reaching a lot of the youth in the country, and I wanted the show to be seen by the youth *especially.* We had a talk where they said they had watched the show and saw that I knew what I was doing in terms of production. They wanted me to produce series 2 and have it on their platform. *Straight away I wanted to know specifics about the deal.* They said they would push the show to the max to their audience and offer me all the technical assistance I needed. *You, the reader, are reading the same offer from the other urban media company that had approached me for series 1.* I was confident to ask about finance and if the company would be willing to fund the production. As per usual when it comes down to *'money'* people get funny and their speech starts to change. They said that what they were trying to do at the time was launch a new channel tailored towards comedy, and as it was at its baby stages in production they had no funds to fund any show, but down the line there would be funding for future series. This I could understand, but in my head I was battling with what to do, as they themselves even said that I would need to close my YouTube channel down.

As their brand was very reputable, after careful consideration, I agreed and said let's do this! The guy I met asked me to let him know once I was at the stages of getting ready to film the series. I was confident that I made a great decision and told the entertainment lawyer what had happened and he too said it was a good move *depending on terms and conditions of contract, of course.* I got straight to the planning of the second series. I sat down with my two little brothers and got their feedback and opinions, which *was similar to when I originally started planning for the pilot.* After I had gotten the notes I needed, I now knew what was going to be happening for each character. The next meaty stage was writing!

Three weeks into writing, enthusiastic and overly creative as I was, I received an email from somebody else who was working at the urban media company whom I just had a meeting with weeks ago. He asked me to come in so we could have a discussion about the show. *I thought this was very odd as the meeting had already happened before, why would another one be needed?* It turned out that he was now in charge of the comedy department. Once again, I was in the building but this time the vibe was *different*, I was very confused and wanted answers. It started off positive but then I was faced with statements and suggestions that totally clashed with my vision. I was told that unless the following had happened, the show could not be on their platform. I'll list the demands for you:

1) Cast members that play the parents MUST be replaced by known actors
2) All scripts must be overlooked by him and another person to 'co-write' in order to 'qualify' for broadcast
3) He must be present on set of filming to make suggestions on cast performance as a 'co-director'

I remember sitting there thinking *"you are having a f****** laugh!"* He reiterated that if the show was going to be on their platform, it had to be hot! *Clearly this guy had underestimated me* so in defence, I told him a breakdown of the journey I've had and that this was a multiple award winning show already. I also told him the cast members I have, I wouldn't think of changing, because there's a statement that I'm making to the industry about the use and idea of *'fresh talent'.* In terms of scripts, I told him my only compromise would be for him to look at the script and I will then decide if his suggestions will work. I was totally against him being on set as a co-director, as this show was solely my vision. No one could tell my story but myself. He said that through him I would be able to get access to certain artists that I wouldn't be able to otherwise. He asked me to go away and think about it over the weekend.

For about a few days my head was heavy and filled with disappointment. *What had happened in the space of three weeks since the first meeting where everything was fine?* I thought it was cheeky of him making all those demands and not offering any money to fund the production. I contacted my friend Aniya who worked in production design on the show *'Misfits'* and told her the situation. She was supportive and totally against going with them, she reminded me how well I had done independently already. There was a part of me that wanted to go with the company because I was literally at a stage where I didn't know what to do, but another part of me wasn't willing to give into their demands. The decision was so tough to make, and I sat there thinking about all the reasons why I was doing this, what I wanted to achieve from it and where I wanted to be from the result of it. Deep within my core I couldn't have anyone put their hands on my work, bearing in mind that if this was a TV network I was dealing with, they would have their say also, so I had to look at both angles. Then again, a TV network would throw money at you - *this company wasn't*. It was for this reason I rejected them! I don't think the guy at the company knows what endless hours of hard work and man power goes into production itself, to be doing this on his demands for free. I sent a professional email telling him series 2 will not be with them.

A shift of energy surged within me as this decision was made and I was back to happy creative mode! Through the grapevine, a woman called Niaz was introduced to me through my young brother. We ended up talking and became good friends. As per usual with any two people that meet they would tell each other what they both did. I knew she was a pilot for an airline and this was very interesting to me as I had never met a pilot before. She was intrigued by my show and saw the first series and loved it. I told her I was in the middle of writing the second series which would be longer episodes. Her daughter who was eight years old at the time was a huge fan of the show also. I told them some funny scenarios that would be featured in the series and they found it very amusing. *I'll talk more about Niaz later.*

Curious about my cast members' availability, I thought it would make sense to contact them to see if they were even available to do a second series. The actress who played 'Angel Mckenzie' goes to school, so the wise thing to do would be to film on a school half-term as I couldn't have her missing days off school. It was a roller coaster schedule with each individual as they were at different points in their lives. Jason (Granddad) and Ria (Charlene) had another production going on in the evenings, so I had to organise according to their schedules during half-term. Sheldon (Raymond) was going to be busy filming for the second series of another project. I now had to look at my scripts and think how to explain his absence for the majority of the series as he wasn't available during the set filming dates. Rewrites had to be done and solutions were made. However, any scene to do with him would have to be filmed on a separate day as he only had one day available. Every other cast member was fine. Parallel to the organisation of this, there was a personal situation in my life involving my ex-partner. I wasn't allowed to use my actual daughter in the show, which was upsetting because, personally, I didn't just want a daddy-daughter bond on the show but also on a personal level. *Those of you who have been paying attention to the story in the show can see where I'm coming from, and where the "voice" truly emanates from.*

Payments, fees etc. - I wanted cast to be paid this time as I felt they had earned it, *seeing as we were now a multiple award winning show, and in general because I wanted them to get paid.* Every angle had to be looked at for the series; I wanted to include some known faces on the underground stand-up comedy scene to appear as cameos for two reasons. Firstly, to help them out into the acting world and, secondly, to increase my audience. Luckily, I knew an artist called 'Mr Cee' whom I had met at the beginning stages of series 1. I reached out to him and he was definitely interested in getting involved. He also stated that if there was any other comedian I was interested in to contact him. *This was very promising and rewarding to know!* I reached out to another comedian called 'Kat Boyce', who is another interesting character I knew from 2010 when I met him at a film screening for

Gladesmore Community School's film *'Value Life'*, which I starred in. He was the host for the screening and *boy did he make me laugh!* I hit him up on Twitter and spoke to him about featuring in the series, and he was over the moon, as he loved the first show! There was one artist called 'Shabba' whom I discovered was the brother of a friend of mine. Mr Cee sent out my request to an artist called 'Slim' who is big in the stand-up comedy scene and Slim was interested. I had to go via his manager to get through to him. There were a few artists I tried to reach out to, but they were either not available or asking for too much money. At this stage, it was literally *"can you work for free?"* as there was not yet any funding. My priority was getting the interest of artists and then figuring a way out for finances. *Note to reader - I was still not working earning money.*

Speaking of funding, there was an opportunity to apply for a community grant. The requirement was that if I involved youth in the community on my project I could be eligible for a £5000 grant! It was up to me to figure out a way of including youth in the production process of the McKenzies. Work experience was my angle to advertise for the funding. I could let youth get work experience by shadowing the different departments: camera, lights, and sound etc. I was also willing to throw in some drama workshops to help out up and coming actors in the community. I applied under BentaVision and ended up having a meeting with a woman called 'Jennifer'. After telling her about me and the work I've done for TV she was excited. She had no idea someone in the borough had worked for major TV shows. She said I was like a celebrity in the community, *I sat there and laughed.* The meeting was very promising and it was also an opportunity to mention filming locations. Jennifer was a resident involvement officer and was responsible for anything to do with filming and the involvement of residents. During this series, there was going to be an episode based on an estate, so an estate was one of my requests. She introduced me to a guy called Alex who was the chairman of a housing association who was all for the idea, and he asked me to meet him one day so I could have a look at the estate. He was a cool guy and the estate looked brilliant for what I had planned... Take a look...

(Pics of estate)

Alex and I got into a deep discussion, as part of the application I had to write down what the money would be spent on. This ranged from equipment, cast, and I thought it would be great to include a screening. £5000 was not going to be enough but it was a start, and I had to budget according to that sum. I was told in the form that it was the maximum price available, but I had to think big and maximise it as much as possible. Alex helped with the application and he included the housing association on it to help boost my chances of getting funding. What convinced me I was going to get the funding was when he told me that no one has ever rejected his requests for money. There was a nearby community centre that he owned, and he said it was also possible to use this as a potential filming location. This vibrated with me because I was in need of a location for the 'speed dating' scene and to use it for a green room for cast to wait when not filming. I now considered this as concrete in my mind that these locations were nothing to worry about. Alex did tell me that there was currently construction work happening on the estate and he promised me that with where I wanted to film, this would not be a problem. The application was filled out and sent back to Jennifer to forward to the decision makers. Fingers crossed.

I was contacted by Frankie's manager who wanted to talk to me about Frankie. I was concerned as to why, but before she got into the discussion, she asked where I was at with the show and if there was anything she could do. *I wouldn't say no to help, as I was doing the work of a whole production office equivalent to 12 staff members!* There was an episode that required a restaurant, which was still a void for me. She told me she knew the owner of a restaurant which had recently opened that wouldn't mind a bit of promotion. She said she would reach out to him and get back to me and send me some pictures in due course. Meanwhile, I was going through all the scripts as casting was to be taken into consideration. Seeing as I wasn't allowed to use my daughter in the show, I needed a replacement. Thank God for Aniya who knew a friend who had a 3-year-old daughter! Aniya and I went out one day so I could meet the mother and the child. She was too cute and very advanced for her age as she spoke quite fluently. The mum was happy for me to use her daughter in the show. *That was that out the way, I didn't really know how I was going to solve that one to be honest.* Because the child had changed from my own daughter to someone else, I had to change the 'Annika' actress from series 1 and find someone who would look more like the child I now had. *Do you remember back when I did the McKenzies pilot, I spoke about an actress who played Annika who had family dramas and couldn't do the series? This was now the Annika for series 2! So, to sum up the madness, she was Annika in the pilot, not in series 1, and she returned for series 2! Crazy huh?*

Like the first series, I posted a casting call on a couple of websites. There were a lot of cast members to audition as this series was going to be huge! I needed a place to hold auditions, but before I looked into it, I needed a breather as the workload was big. I was still finalizing scripts, sorting out locations and I hadn't yet even planned how I was going to shoot the series or know any of my lines from the actor perspective! I needed help so I reached out to a woman I met ages ago at a screening whose name was Scarlett. I knew I needed an extra pair of hands and wanted her to assist with casting. Her services would have required a lot of money though as she was going to help out with various areas in the production, but I didn't think too much about that as I was certain funding would come through for the community grant. She made a few calls, and came back with a church that had an open room available to use for free - this was brilliant! It did require me going down to the church to check it over and meet with the woman who looked after it first, *so she knew what the show and I were all about etc.* An agreement was made and I planned dates of auditions, which were beneficial for both of us.

Back at home after hours and late nights of scrolling through actors that had applied, I was now shortlisting. As I was doing this, a girl called Shamara called me up and asked if I was looking for any help, so I looked at her CV. She offered to help me if I only paid for her expenses. This appealed to me as she was immediately available and offered a lower price and was offering more work than Scarlett. I need to mention here, I knew of Shamara because she interviewed me on a radio station when I did Eastenders E20, so we already had more than an acquaintance. A decision had to be made and I tried various attempts at calling Scarlett but wasn't getting through. It resulted in me turning her down on Facebook, which didn't go quite so well. Put it this way, the last thing I heard from her was this...

> I've been calling you all day yesterday and today Samuel.
> As I said, no big deal, it's just when I commit to something, I commit. I free my calendar, and rearrange things. This sometimes is why I am often reluctant to work with the black community, it's no big deal for you, but I rearranged my diary according to the dates you gave me.

I thought it was funny and rude considering Scarlett was 'black' herself, and it showed me deep down her true characteristics, so I think it was best that I did leave her alone as she could have proven detrimental to the project in the long run. The good thing about that experience was that I ended up getting casting space out of it for free. It's funny how these things work out!

I received news from Alex the chairman of the housing association, which left me devastated. It turned out that I was not going to be eligible for the community grant of £5000 as I wasn't an organization - I was an individual. I was vexed because he knew this from day 1 when I first met him and he originally told me it was ok as long as his association was on the application form! I couldn't believe it! *What was wrong in doing a project which would benefit people in the community?! What was wrong in a young person like me stepping up to do something amazing?! It goes to show that there's always someone who has a last say and I was just about sick of this now! This made me want to further stick to the independent route, after all, the community people did not want to help someone that had been an inspiration to people, that was a recognizable face from television. What the hell was I to do now with absolutely no money? I did not want to do this again on no money due to the content of the scripts and the people I wanted involved.* No, I said that this series was going to be the seed that gave birth to everything I ever wanted in my life! Alex told me that even though I wasn't eligible for the funding; I could still film on the estate and in the community centre.

Crying in my room, head under pillow and wanting to lock off the world, I was trying my best to hold on to the faith that this show was going to get done regardless; I continued to refine the scripts. A thought crossed my mind about a time I met Levi Roots when I facilitated a drama workshop with some kids in the community, this was ages ago nearer the time of series 1. I had mentioned to him back then that I was doing the show and thought it might interest him in terms of product placement and sponsorship. I didn't hear back from him then but maybe now was a better time to contact him. I literally came up with a plan and researched how I could benefit his brand with my show seeing as they were both Caribbean. After hours of putting together a document I emailed his PA, it was worth a try. I couldn't let this be my only source as I knew that it wouldn't be immediate that I would hear a response. Luckily, I knew the head of Marketing for Adidas and thought to try there to see if there were funds I could get through them with my show and possibly advertising the Adidas brand. The lady had told me that they don't fund shows, only events, but she did say that I could have some clothes from Adidas. I was grateful and thought that this would help the relationship for future opportunities. Up to this day, I have never heard back from Levi Roots.

One day I went to Niaz's house (*the woman I mentioned before that my brother introduced me to).* I was writing more of the script at her house and she was asking me about my show and its updates. I had told her about the disappointment with the community grant and she asked me roughly how much a great series like this would cost? I told her the story of my journey with the pilot and the first series and she saw that I had done a lot on no money. I explained to her what I was trying to achieve. With the extent that I wanted, I gave a bold figure of £20,000. She laughed and said she would give me £10,000 to fund the show and make it happen. *You the reader know that I was overjoyed with this!* There was a condition though - when I make it big I must pay her back and give her VIP access to all my premieres. I said "DEAL!"

Now the show was really on. I was researching a great sound recorder, and one of the characters in the script required an American accent. I thought to go all out and fly out an actress from LA to be in the show! *Remember when I went to the HBFF in 2011 and I met a girl called Tyra Richards who also supported me at the LA Web Festival award ceremony?* I said to myself that I was going to send her a surprise Facebook message asking her if she wanted to fly out and do the show. Tyra was flattered and over the moon, she had never been to London before and it made it feel rewarding to me. I asked her to send me an audition tape online and we would go from there. Her tape was flawless and I knew I had made a right decision. The only thing that had to be sorted out was going through her SAG union as it was yet to be decided if 'All About The McKenzies' was SAG eligible. After endless back and forth emails, SAG accepted a New Media agreement to be signed in order to allow Tyra to do the project. With this all done I booked her flight! I felt this show was on a next level now that she was flying over here.

(Pic of me and Tyra)

With all scripts complete and actors shortlisted, it was time to do the auditions. There were two days that were booked in January. Shamara assisted me during the process by acting as receptionist, dealing with actors as and when they came in. Israr attended one of the days to record the process. All sorts of personalities and different qualities came through the door. Now I can understand from the actor point of view why directors and writers sometimes are not in attendance at auditions and would rather watch tapes - it takes a lot out of you! Some actors inspired me to create different characters within the series and I ended up writing extra parts with that actor in mind. *What can I say, I'm a nice guy!* Now I had every audition filmed for me to watch again when I got home to decide who was getting what. Casting was fun but very tiring! You'll notice in series 2 there's a character called 'Ian'. He was originally supposed to be white but I couldn't find any actor suitable to play the role. I even reached out to a couple of white stand-up comedians, but they either were unavailable or not interested. I ended up giving the role to an actor I personally knew who was black. His name was Adrian and we go way back through the years as we attended drama classes together. That's where we met. In fact, if you think back to the first series, do you remember the casting director? The actress who played her was also within the same circle as Adrian and I, and she did the makeup for the cast for this series, so it was a great reunion!

Proud as I was, I knew this series was going to be a massive hit, as I made sure every ingredient was in the show to make it taste nice. For the finale episode, I wanted it to be huge! By looking at cast interviews for series 1, I remembered that Fenella who plays 'Delia' mentioned she wanted to do dance and never had the chance. This gave me the idea to include dancing in this series but on another level- *I had to go all out!* I advertised for dancers online, but wasn't receiving any major responses. Aniya was good friends with a man called 'Turbo' who is quite big on the dancing scene. He is a judge with Alesha Dixon on a BBC show. Aniya contacted him and asked if he could send out a message to all his dancers. I was very grateful for this and saw this show panning out nicely and said Aniya would be co-producer. A date was made for auditions to be held at Fitness First gym in Leyton, London. According to Aniya we had about six dance crews confirmed for attendance. *This was so exciting! I felt like a little kid who was going to get an ice-cream.* Turbo was a bit late, but I made sure I set up the gym for auditions to take place. When he finally turned up he was asking me the kind of things I was looking for and we got on very well. Time went by and no dancers had turned up. Turbo was on the phone calling them up and they said they were on their way. I was stressing out as per usual as I looked at the clock and we had about 30 minutes left until the gym wanted their space back. To kill time Turbo was dancing to various songs as I stood there admiring and filming him. At the back of my mind was, *'when the hell are these dancers going to turn up?'* Disappointed that no dancers had turned up, which was a waste of time, the last thing I wanted to do was axe the dancing as I thought it added a whole new dynamic to the show.

Only a week to go to go till filming started and I had some serious concerns as I had discovered someone who was supposed to be a guest part in the show had flown out to another country and never told me, which was very unprofessional, and this actor needed to be replaced. The actress who played the head teacher in the first series also told me that she wouldn't be available for this series as she was in another country as there were family issues going on that needed her attention. Another emergency casting had to be done for the head teacher and, luckily, we found someone who was going to be available and suitable. On a normal production for television, I wouldn't have to be concerned with any of this as there would have been a staff member who would take care of it, but seeing as at this point I only had limited staff, I had to make sure all gaps were filled within the whole production. In Series 1 we had no lighting, but thanks to the funding from Niaz, I was able to hire out equipment! There was a lesson to learn with this though, and make note of this, you cannot hire out any equipment unless your production is insured! These were the words of a producer I used to work with on a commercial for ASOS. I had no idea and I only had a week to sort this out! Luckily, he referred me to a good hire company and insurance broker. I needed to make sure my production had employee liability insurance, as this would protect me if a cast or staff member got injured or even killed on the production, also the protection of crew's equipment if they were to use their own, so it was worth having.

With equipment in place, crew hired, cast member positions filled, and locations sorted. It was time for the first day of filming which took place January 20th 2013. It was snowing heavily and I was up at 5.30am ready to go! I was excited to see the cast members again as I hadn't seen them for about a year since the first series! My concern was everyone getting to the location safely in all the snow. There were two locations to film in and they were very near each other. I was grateful for the help of Niaz who volunteered to cater for the whole production making sure everybody was fed by providing breakfast and lunch. By meeting a person like this I can say that I was being looked after by the universe! Aniya and Shamara too were gems in the whole process. Shamara volunteered to use my camcorder and film behind the scenes for the whole series! *You'll later find out Shamara was a girl of many talents in various aspects of the production.* Aniya, as creative as she is, put hours of her energy into the making of props etc. and she did a fantastic job! As I'm talking about her it brings to my attention that I completely forgot Aniya hooked me up with a music producer called 'Nutty P', who was responsible for providing the music for the dance off for the finale episode, and a hip-hop violinist for the restaurant episode.

Alex, the chairman of the housing association contacted me. Do you remember he told me about the construction work on the estate? Well guess what? The builders told him that the areas I wanted to use were going to be unavailable as they were now setting up scaffolding all around that part of the estate. This info was relayed to me during the day of filming! It was a challenge to stay focused knowing at the back of my mind that needed to be sorted.

(Areas on estate available for filming...)

What also didn't help was when moving to the second location I had a car crash! My car skidded in the road due to the ice and hit a lamppost. There was a dent on the side of the car but I had to keep telling myself the show must go on. I was driving in third gear to the location. 'Sheldon', who plays Raymond McKenzie, was only available on this day as he had another project, so if I wanted this series to make sense, all personal feelings about my car had wait. On a day off from filming, I looked on the casting call for dancers and saw that there was a dance crew who were interested in dancing for the show. By looking at their videos on YouTube, I knew I didn't need to audition them, plus at this point I was desperate and needed someone. A girl dance group contacted me, I remember watching their performance at the BEFFTA Awards and they were happy to be involved at such last minute. I classed this day as tying up loose ends to make sure I had solutions for everything that had occurred so far.

There was a total of 12 shooting days ranging from 12-14hr shoots and me having 3 hour sleeps between each! I'm not going to bore you with the specifics of each day, but I shall explain some other important aspects and challenges that came with it.

FURTHER OBSTACLES

- The sound engineer got injured one evening when he was looking for another battery for his sound pack. He had ducked under a light and it caught his head. The light had ripped some of the skin off of his head and it was bleeding. I had to stop the whole production and run out to get a first aid kit immediately. A lesson to learn, always have a first aid kit on set and thank God for the insurance, otherwise I could have been screwed if he decided to take it further.

- One of the dancers got injured as they attempted to do a cartwheel and slipped and hurt their hand; luckily it wasn't anything of a serious nature.
- During filming one day, the memory card for the camera got corrupted and no files could be retrieved from everything we shot. We had to reshoot everything we did for the morning resulting in delaying the production dramatically! Not to mention the actors' frustration.
- The episode where we filmed the armed police, although this was a funny experience, it was very serious. The actors had guns and a uniform that looked real. We were filming on private property in a secluded garage where resident's cars were parked. There was a resident who drove in during a take and saw the armed officers and immediately reversed back out not looking where he was driving, and nearly knocked into the brick wall. Another resident had called the police as she thought there was something dodgy going on. Luckily, the costume hire company had an ex-police officer present to monitor what we were doing, otherwise we would have all got arrested.
- The restaurant owner turned up over 1 hour late to open up the premises. I had cast and crew standing in the freezing cold waiting. He said he had *"slept*

in". It's important to know that at times like these, remain professional and calm. Easier said when done considering when you have a time to wrap by.

- When filming on one of the house locations, a cast member broke the owner's chair and had to be replaced out of the show's budget. I'm yet to know if I'll be allowed to use that house again for the next series as the owner was not impressed!
- In the hospital, we ended up being there two hours later than scheduled and this resulted in the hospital charging the production double what they asked.
- Lights got blown on a couple of filming days, but luckily spare bulbs were on standby.
- Grandad's makeup had run out one day on set and I had to call up Sarah (makeup artist) to travel to all sorts of locations to find the hair for granddad's beard. Without the beard continuity, would have been a serious issue for the show.
- At the end of the day filming at the school, my time was up as the students needed to go home. I had to literally beg the teacher to allow me 15 more minutes to finish up. Luckily, they granted me my wish and the day was completed.
- 3 weeks before the launch of the second series, my music composer sent me an email stating that he could no longer continue with the project as he had relationship troubles and got fired from his day job, leaving me in a predicament of an already established launch and no finished product *(at this point I only had music for a trailer, title sequence and end credits but none for the entire series*). I was unable to find anyone else as there was no budget

for it. It resulted on me threatening legal action on him as he had already been paid for the job in advance. Thankfully, a day after things had resolved on his end and he continued with the project. Little did I know I was going to get a phone call the same day saying that his MIDI keyboard had broken and he needed a new one. I had to meet with him the next day and drive with him to the music shop to get another one – Madness, hey?

- My car during the last couple of weeks had an engine problem and was not fit for driving on the road. The mechanics said it would cost around £700 plus VAT. I had no car for a few days and didn't know when I would be able to pay for it. Niaz came to the rescue and sorted it for me, this woman was an angel!

On wrap of the second series, I knew in my gut that the show had exceeded its expectations and I was proud. I guess you could say my whole life for the last two and a half years was literally dedicated to one idea. I was making sure that every component was perfect, making sure every episode spoke to a certain someone in the world, making sure my cast members were seen in the best light for their growth, making sure I went against the stereotype that the world portrays, overall I was making sure I had a fun, innovative, energetic universal show for families to sit down and enjoy! Like any production that you work on, after filming had finished it was a very emotional time, it was like there was a huge void because the whole x number of months was preparation for the filming, and then it's over. All that was left to do, was make sure that all the artwork was created, the website was built, the show was edited, and the music was composed.

Although I oversee all aspects of production, there was nothing meaty left for me to do.

After reviewing the rough cuts, it revealed a lot to me about a universal law called *'gratitude'*. Looking at all clips, and everyone that was involved gave me a joyful feeling. As without those people and their contributions, there wouldn't be anything for me to look at on my laptop screen. Everything from cast, crew, locations, even the meetings I had, all led up to the end product. A lot of people say to me that I am hard on myself, they even say that I don't celebrate my achievements- I guess this is true and it's something that I need to work on myself. I guess when you are taking on the pressures and responsibilities of wearing a lot of hats it takes more out of you than if you were just the actor. I have so much respect for every production that takes place, as I know what it takes for a show to take off. A rocket when it takes off uses 70% of its energy to get into the air, but once it's in the air it's only 30%. A Chinese bamboo tree once a seed is sown, grows its roots, and germinates for 5 years before it shoots through the ground where everyone can see it.

So, what now after all filming and editing is done? Well, things had to be done differently, as this time I wanted the whole world to see this show. Hard-core marketing was needed but deep within me, I knew I wanted some sort of financial return, as for the last two and a half years I had made no money unless it was a commercial job I got from my agent. I was grateful enough to have my parents and a good friend sustain me whilst I was working on the bigger agenda, otherwise I don't know how I would have coped. So how was I going to make money from this? The one thing that was bothering me was figuring out a way to sell my show online. YouTube was free but there was no facility that allowed people to pay for watching videos. After some research, I was introduced to 'Vimeo-on-demand', which is a service Vimeo has where creators can sell their work and sell it on their own website, using the technology that Vimeo has. This was my opportunity to show people my worth and value my content, as I believed that what I had created was worth paying to see, no different than going to the cinema to watching a movie. How much to charge? Well, I spent ages thinking about that because I wanted it to be affordable, but at the same time I didn't want to be cheap as I had put in some serious overtime and energy into creating the show. Human behaviour shows that we will always jump to freebies, but hadn't I done the first series as a freebie? It was time to make some money and I even went as far as letting everyone see the first episode of the new series for FREE just to entice them as to what the rest of the series would be like. A technique I used for the editing process was at the end of the episode have a short snippet of what to expect in the next, which would be enough for everyone to get excited and purchase the series.

Throughout the recent years of my life I have always wanted to pierce through the veil and do something different other than sharing videos on social network sites, tweeting etc. I enjoy the cinema and I love when I walk in and look at the huge posters on the wall and thinking to myself that'll one day it will be my movie. This was a light-bulb moment, and I looked around and saw that lots of people visit the cinema daily of all age ranges. What if I had a poster of the new series advertised in the cinema foyer? Come to think of it, no one I knew who had a web-series had EVER done that. This would be a great way to promote the show to people who have never heard of me other than my Facebook friends and twitter followers! People suffer due to lack of knowledge, and a common misperception people have about advertising is that it would cost hundreds and thousands of pounds because big Oscar winning movies advertise in there so it must be very expensive. Then people don't even give it further thought. I did a bit of research and found a company called 'Primesight' who deal with outdoor advertising and I was blown away at the price to advertise in a cinema. It was a lot cheaper than hundreds of thousands of pounds. Put it this way, the price does vary depending on the area the cinema is in. But with the cinemas I wanted, let's just say it cost a few hundred. After more research, I then had another "aha" moment, what about billboard advertising? How much would this cost? Once again it depends on size and location. When thinking location, I was wondering where my market was. The prices for billboards were more expensive than the cinema advertising but shockingly affordable! There was budget for two billboards and two cinema boards, I picked the locations and ordered it with further funds from Niaz. A minimum campaign is two weeks when you choose to go through these outdoor advertising companies. The graphics designer for the show had a lot of work to do.

A billboard poster in Wembley (London)

The McKenzies website was up and running, www. allaboutthemckenzies.com. I made sure the website had looked very professional and fun and easily navigational. I wanted to start building a list of subscribers who would eventually become customers. I had seen companies do this before where they have their website and allow people to type in their emails for subscribing- this way they can always send out group emails to their lists. I would want everyone to stay updated, and I would want to know specifics about the people who watch my show, as this would help for potential services and just to see 'who' is a fan!

Youth Media of the Month May 2013

Surprises and "good luck" seemed to always come my way. Before I was going to launch the Mckenzies online I met up with my production assistant in April 2013 and had a meeting about how we could best promote the show, she brought to my attention the Youth Media Agency. I never knew who these people were but she did, so she said she would introduce me in an email. The Youth Media Agency is the national home for UK youth media, they deal with raising the profile of over 300 media platforms, they deliver campaign and media training working with 16-25 year olds. I was 26 at that time but they were willing to have a meeting with me anyway.

The Youth Media Agency was based in Kings Cross in London and I told the agency what I was about and what I was looking to do. They were very impressed by the journey I had, and on the spot, they wanted me to be youth media of the month for May 2013! You may be wondering what I mean by "youth media of the month"? What that means is that for a whole month they will promote you through their website and find other avenues to get you out there to the public to raise your profile. This was brilliant because they also wanted to help me with doing a launch for my show for when it came out. Susanna, the youth media agency director said that a few people owed her favours at the Rich Mix Cinema in Shoreditch and that there was a possibility of the event happening there. After more venue research, we ended up getting the greenlight for the event to go ahead at the Rich Mix. Now it was time for invites, which included my own contacts plus theirs.

The date was set for it to happen May 13th 2013, which was a month away from where we were. It was going to be a free event for Youth Media and mainstream only, so not open to the public. See the invite below:

The show was due to go live May 3rd 2013 on YouTube *(I thought it was best to at least have episode 1 on YouTube to entice people to buy the rest of the series on Vimeo.)* I made up my mind to charge people 69p per episode. I thought this was very affordable and would be acceptable to anyone, after all most people shop at the 99p store! I wasn't being cheap about the price; I just took into consideration who the show mainly appealed to and priced accordingly. Remember, I didn't know how it was going to turn out online as this was a brand-new direction for me to take the show and I wanted to see some sort of return. On the night of the launch it was packed out, and about 150 people showed up, I was so happy *(I never had a show launch before and this was a show that I created).* Mr Cee and Kat Boyce were the hosts for the night as they featured in the first episode of the show and they certainly knew how to make the audience laugh. Interviews were being held and various youth media showed up. It is a great feeling when you see the fruits of your labour come together to work for the greater good all in one room and view your show on a cinema screen! I had T-shirts created, pens, flyers, fridge magnets, posters, and keyrings to give away in goodie bags. I had a speech at the end and thanked everybody for coming and told them to look into the show online when it was out (at this point episode 1 was on YouTube).

A collage of the All About The McKenzies Launch at the Rich Mix Cinema May 2013, Courtesy of Youth Media Agency.

So how were the sales of All About The McKenzies going online? what was the progress? VERY MINIMAL! Hardly anyone was buying my show online- I was gutted! After all I went through, all that planning, all that filming and NO ONE was buying my show online. It cost 69p and no one could invest and pay me for my time, hard work, and effort?! I felt unappreciated, used and was at a point that I felt like people didn't deserve my talents. My sales mounted up to about $40 (£28) and I had to think long and hard about what to do.

On a side note, I think that social networking sites and YouTube have numbed the minds of individuals to an extent that people don't want or expect to pay for anything anymore- as soon as they see a price or that you are trying to sell something to them, they run! I simply put everything I had into my show with the use of someone else's money to see if I could finally make a return on something I put 3 years of my life into! This experience showed me a lot about the mindset of humanity when it comes to being online, even my closest friends did not purchase the series and I was very concerned. Why was it so hard to get paid for what you love doing? The price of the show was the same price of a packet of crisps and cheaper than the 99p store - there were no excuses. I couldn't just have my show sitting collecting dust so I had to eventually release them on YouTube FOR FREE! Believe me when I say that all of a sudden, the viewers came out the woodwork, why? IT WAS FREE! Everyone was enjoying the show more than ever, but all I could think of was *"I'm not earning any money from this..."*

Soon I was going to be put out of my misery because I received a surprise phone call from Susanna one day, who had said to me that she had gotten off the phone with a woman called Jane, who enquired about what the Youth Media Agency was. Luckily at the time I was still Youth Media of the month and Susanna explained to Jane that she should check out my stuff. After I got off the phone with Susanna I researched who this woman was and to my awe this was a *serious* woman who had done lots for professional media and TV. I was buzzing and told Susanna to pass Jane my details. After a lengthy conversation with Jane, I got more background into what was happening. A new TV channel was going to be launching in 2014 called 'London Live', and Jane was in charge of it. London Live is backed by the Evening Standard and The Independent and they had just been given a licence to have a network. Jane was seeking content for her channel, hence the reason she contacted Susanna in the first place. She requested a meeting and I agreed.

All I could say was 'wow' when I looked around me being in the headquarters of the Evening Standard, Daily Mail, Independent and other top newspapers for London. This had to be the next possible biggest step for me. In the meeting was Jane and another lady who dealt with Acquisitions for the channel, *(for those of you who don't know what acquisitions is, they basically deal with buying and managing shows and films for transmission for a network).* I found out in this meeting that this other lady, named Jay, was the woman responsible for nearly 98% of all the American programming on British Television such as: Sex in the City, Lost, Desperate Housewives, Prison Break and much more. If any of you have seen those programmes on TV, I was sitting right next to the woman responsible for you even knowing about them. Prior to the meeting, I had sent Jane links to the whole series to check it out. To cut a long story short, London Live wanted All About The McKenzies! I had mixed emotions about this because although I was happy, I wanted to know what all the terms and conditions were going to be etc. The beauty of the matter was, the series 2 of All About The McKenzies was made to TV broadcasting standards, so the show was already made. They were in a position for me to license it to them, and were asking me how much I was selling it for. I had told them that I would speak to my lawyer and get back to them. What they also said was that they wanted to do a deal with me that was different than how networks operate in general. They knew that I wasn't an established production company then, and they said they were willing to take a risk with me because they saw that series 2 was of a high standard *(remember before I started writing series 2? Didn't I say that I was going to write longer episodes for TV broadcast length as I had learned from the networks that rejected me before? Didn't it pay off in the end?).* They also wanted to do a development deal with me on a completely different project of whatever ideas I had! I left the meeting and was over the moon! A TV network wanted MY SHOW! They were impressed with the quality of the programming and scriptwriting that they wanted to broadcast what I had done. I demanded an urgent meeting with my lawyer.

Here's when I was going to be experiencing what business in TV was all about... *bear in mind, reader, that I had never gone down this path before.* I remember reflecting on the whole journey I have had with this show and this was the highest peak yet! I felt that this was the right move, but security for my show kept popping up in my mind. I wanted to know the ins and outs of how this whole thing worked. It may have been a great opportunity but I wanted to protect my show. I had the meeting with London Live in May 2013, and it took months when my lawyer and their lawyer were playing chess with contracts. My lawyer is seeking out for my best interests and their lawyer is seeking for their best interests. I always thought the term *"it's just business"* was a joke- a line that they use in movies before they kill someone, but during this 4 month process it was daunting. It was like I wanted the deal but at the same time I didn't want to sacrifice certain things, so it was all about negotiation and kind of like the game show 'Deal or No Deal'. Don't get me wrong readers, they have no power to change anything in my show because it's already done, as I can still continue with my roles of producer, writer, director, and actor. The beast was in the small print of the contract, but luckily, I have to give thanks to Mary otherwise I wouldn't have met my current Lawyer who is excellent at what he does. One of London Live's terms was that episode

2-6 of series 2 was to be removed offline, but I could keep episode 1 on there. The deal was signed and All About The McKenzies would be on TV in 2014.

To check out the second series of All About The McKenzies, type in YouTube: All About The Mckenzies series 2, or if you are reading an ebook click here.

CHAPTER 5

KEEP ON KEEPING ON! - SERIES 3

By now, can you actors see what can happen after you make one decision? Please don't be overwhelmed as I understand it can be a lot to take in. Most of this book may seem like it's all about me sharing a story but there's a reason you need to see the process. You'll understand more about that as you continue to read.

I knew a next series had to be done. February 2014 was the new goal of filming of series 3 of 'All About The McKenzies'. By now I knew what to expect; I knew what to prepare for as I was a lot more experienced from the previous series. London Live was due to launch in a couple of months, and they already had the content from series 2 that was going be shown across the TV screens of London. Niaz agreed to up the budget from what we had on the second series, so we were due to have more money. This was going to be the meatiest series yet! Six episodes were written and I made sure that it was going to be better than the last. With pre-production, everything went smoothly: scripts were written and this time I did something I hadn't done before. I arranged a script readthrough with the whole cast. *For those reading this who are unaware, script readthroughs are when an entire series has been written, and you get in a room with all your cast and have them read the scripts together. This is a fun process, and it is also a great tool to use to identify what works and doesn't work within a script. Sometimes actors can bring something totally different to the table, and you get ideas from them, which works out better for the writing. It's also a nice way for the team to gel before they see each other on set, especially if they are actors that haven't met before.*

Feeling very humbled and excited with great expectations knowing that filming was happening in 3 weeks' time, one evening I was treated to a theatre play by one of my friends. We went to the Hackney Empire and watched a pantomime, 'Puss in Boots' that a mutual friend was performing in. Ironically, it was Kat Boyce who starred in series 2 of the show as an armed police officer. I knew this play was going to be a lot of jokes! I remember it being just over halfway through the play when I received an email on my phone and my heart sank. It was Niaz who said she wouldn't be able to fund the series. *Reader, please bear in mind that we were supposed to be filming in 3 weeks.* I left the pantomime with my friend and I was going crazy! So many thoughts were racing through my head. Niaz had family issues, and it would require most of the show's budget to sort out. Although I understood the circumstances, I had come too far for this to happen. I tried calling her, but she wasn't picking up. Everything I had planned, the schedules, the location, the filming, the casting, everything was under jeopardy at this moment, and I knew this was not a quitting situation!

Eventually, I got hold of her and managed to meet up at her house on a later day. She told me the whole story. I just sat there and listened. As she spoke, I asked myself what the next step was and how this could be resolved. We were there for a few hours when another one of her friends came around. Together, we discussed the budget and ways we could make the show work to the budget that was leftover. Sacrifices had to be made and the script had to be rejigged. After a few hours of budgeting and weighing against the scripts, what was meant to be the budget originally was now cut down to under half of what was agreed. This was still more money than series 2 but I had to make sure that the series would work for the new budget we now had. I cannot stress to you how 'on the spot' I was with this; the whole production was riding on getting this resolved otherwise it wasn't going to happen. The great thing was, a solution was found and heartbeats were restored to the normal pulsations.

It was on! The filming dates had arrived and I still had my original crew. However, there was a new addition with new technology. We welcomed a guy called Allessandro, who was an amazing asset as he provided Steadicam and gave us value with most of our shots for filming *(up to this point I never experienced using Steadicam in a production unless I was acting in someone else's).* He was also looking to do more work in the film industry in this country; most of his resume was for work in Italy. I found him online at Mandy.com. During the post production phase, I worked with a different music composer called Jamie who was absolutely awesome! I also found him on the same website. What I did to select who was going to be the composer was advertise and state that I was going to make my decision based on who could compose the best to an older series 2 episode. After reviewing the applicants and their compositions, I found Jamie.

The second day of filming, we were filming at a restaurant In Leytonstone. This was a day of serious pressure as we had a lot of extras and we had a certain period to be out of the restaurant. As a producer, you need to think creatively because anything can happen on the day including one of your actors getting arrested. Yes, that's right! Adrian who played the character 'Ian' got arrested the night before, and was released on the day of filming, but didn't arrive until later in the day. I had to rearrange scenes and write him out of a scene on the spot to keep the flow moving. I won't mention the reasons for the arrest. The important thing here is that you see how the problem was addressed and resolved.

Time was getting on and it was against us. The manager of the restaurant came in about 5pm when we were meant to be out! He was concerned because customers were due to be in the restaurant within the hour, but I still had scenes to film! It got to a stage where customers were coming in and we were still filming. The good thing is that we were in the VIP section of the restaurant, but the noise from the customers travelled to where we were filming, it was so frustrating! Luckily, Niaz with her female touch went to speak to the manager and buttered him up with her charm to allow us to finish. ALWAYS HAVE A FLIRTACIOUS FEMALE CREW MEMBER WHO CAN DEAL WITH DIFFICULT MALE MANAGER! - No joke!

The next day was a day off and I was tired from the previous night, but relieved that we got those scenes in the can. What a roller coaster! I said that today was the day of relaxation and contemplation of the whole journey. I was proud of myself for what I had achieved; the whole show had come a long way, and we going to be seen on TV in a couple of months. As much as I love roller coasters in theme parks, having that as your metaphor for life can be unexpected as you don't know when the next loop the loop will rear its head. As I was sitting in my bed staring at the McKenzies poster on the wall, my phone vibrated with a text. Remember that loop the loop I spoke about? It was here. I got a text from the dad character saying that he can't do the show any more! WHAT?! Are you insane?! We were only 3 out of 13 days of filming and there was no way in hell I was going to allow a cast member to do this to me after so much money and time had gone into it. I immediately called Niaz and told her the situation, she was vexed and contacted the dad character. She then called me back and said that later that night, myself, her, and Sheldon would meet for dinner to discuss. *Personally, there was nothing to discuss because, as far as I was concerned a contract was signed and he had agreed to be in the production for all of his filming days, or I would sue his ass!* But I had to play it cool, as I needed him.

We met that night and he addressed an issue he had from the restaurant, apparently, he didn't like the toilet humour and felt very uncomfortable with it. This was complete nonsense and showed me that he never fully read the scripts, otherwise he would not have had that problem because he knew it was going to happen. What I discovered was that this actor only saw series 1 and never saw series

2 of the show, and his views of it were based on what he originally saw. *This is what annoys me about certain actors, it makes sense to me that if you act in a show, wouldn't you watch it?* He had no idea of what had happened in the previous series and neither did he read the scripts for the current series that we were filming- very unprofessional! I could tell his heart wasn't into the show. In fact, he told me this when he showed up at the readthrough only to tell me that to my face in a separate room. I knew that after what just happened, that was the end of the actor after the series was completed. Why would I have an actor on my show that doesn't really want to be there? After a talk with Niaz and I, he agreed to finish the series.

We got more creative this series with the experience of new technology and ideas. There was one scene with myself and Adrian as police officers, and I acted as two characters in the same scene talking to myself. This was introduced to me through Israr and we thought we'd give it a whirl, look below:

All About The McKenzies Series 3 Episode 1 – Courtesy of BentaVision.

It's important that we creatively think of new ways to engage audiences and produce our content. It's vital that we always strive to be better than we were last time. If we do not change for the better, we remain the same, which means we get boring and stagnated. Creative solutions are key to all obstacles.

I'll give you another example, in episode 6 of series 3, we needed a marquee delivered and set up. Niaz was responsible for taking care of this, and judging by the photographs I saw before the order was made, the size looked perfect. After filming a few days later, I went to check out the Marquee to find that it was too small. My immediate thought was how the scene was going to be filmed in such a small Marquee. I didn't have the answer, but because this was the scene we were going to be doing the next day, I rolled with it and knew we would have to figure it out on the day.

All About The McKenzies Series 3
Episode 6 – Courtesy of BentaVision.

After talking with the crew on the day, Steve the sound guy had a creative solution to make it 'perceived' that the marquee was bigger simply by filming from certain angles, and thus, the scene was filmed. Make use of the resources you have. You may not have a solution but someone else in your crew might have one. There are endless things I can talk about with what can potentially happen on set or off set, but the important thing is to keep going and find solutions for every problem that occurs. This helps you grow and become stronger not just as your role, but you as a person.

I allowed work experience on this series and 3 people could experience being on set and taking part with various roles. I think it's important to allow for work experience because back in the day when I did Eastenders E20 and shadowed the director on the main EastEnders, I learned a lot just by observing. Most productions wouldn't allow for work experience, but I'm all about sharing the knowledge, why? Because I know what it's like to have no support, and have to create something from scratch to get people to notice you exist.

Everything was in the can and two months later London Live launched. It was April 2014, after being on the network I'm sure you can imagine how over the moon I was. I was paid to have my episodes on their channel and it felt great to be *paid,* especially after all my efforts up to this point. London Live was a new channel and 'All About The McKenzies' was the first piece of content that they acquired. This same month, I moved into a flat and used some of my acquisition money. The living room was spacious, it had a master bedroom, a small classy bathroom, and a walkthrough kitchen. I remember going Ikea and buying furniture like a wardrobe, chest of drawers, a bookcase, a computer table etc. I learned to be the DIY type and manually put together all the furniture *(next time I would rather buy furniture ready-made).* I was proud, I felt like I was moving forward, and finally, I was out of mum and dad's house, and it was by doing something *I loved*. I even bought a trampoline because the flat had a back garden. This trampoline was not for me, it was for my daughter whenever I had her come over; she likes gymnastics. One of my warmest moments was a time that I was looking after her. We baked cakes for the first time ever - It was daddy and daughter in the kitchen. I remember laughing at the little apron I bought her, I think she was only 4yrs old at the time. Looking into her eyes gave me flashbacks of my whole experience leading up to that moment. She was one of the main reasons I was persevering in doing this this whole thing.

8.00 The Tube (R).
Behind-the-scenes look at the London Underground, beginning with rail replacement works threatening to disrupt the weekday service, and a woman pushed onto a track.

9.00 Peep Show (R).
Comedy, starring Robert Webb and David Mitchell as misfits with an unhealthy dependence on each other.

9.30 All About the McKenzies.
New series. Samuell and his best friend go speed-dating.

10.00 F2 Kicks Off (R).
Football freestyle pioneers showcase their skills.

10.30 Food Junkies (R).
Cabbie Joey Bone samples three separate pie and mash shops, and a new pop-up restaurant launches in Euston.

11.00 Doc Heads Presents LSD.

I saw newspaper articles in the Evening Standard with the show's picture in it. What made me really smile was looking at London Live's running order for their network in the paper and seeing 'All About The McKenzie's in the line-up.

My show was on TV, I didn't care that it was a new network, it was on TV! Lots of people were proud of me, my family, some of my friends, and what was weird was that some of the webseries creator's attitudes toward me started to change. it was like they were avoiding me, 'likes' and 'shares' on Facebook were not coming from them... what happened? Was it jealousy? This wasn't just about my show, this was about a movement for all of us, especially people of colour. I never really understood why but I made sure that there was no concentration of my energies on it as it would make me not feel good. After conversations with London Live they were willing to acquire series 3 of the show. I sent them private links for them to review. "I finally made my mark", I said to my myself and it was well deserved.

Weird things happened as London Live launched. Very frustratingly, the schedules kept on changing for when Mckenzies was supposed to broadcast. In the newspaper, it would say that it started at 9.30pm, but then it showed at a different time and vice versa. This was confusing not just for me, but the viewers also. I remember having disputes with the network as a lot of work had gone into the making of the episodes for it to be treated like this. Their response was "it was teething problems", so they had to experiment with different time frames.

The show had the highest ratings on their channel for about two months, but it was still not known to the wide public by a lot of people as their main promotion was their newspaper. I felt their strategy for marketing could have been a lot different - they didn't even have adverts for the show! How were people supposed to know about the show if you didn't advertise it with commercials? We had them made, they just never used it.

I noticed that they acquired other YouTube shows as well, I was beginning to see that they were looking to leverage off the YouTube shows followers to increase their audiences. It never worked.

A few months went by, and I hadn't received an answer in regards to the next series of episodes I filmed, whether they were going to acquire it or not. I was very positive, despite the news of the ratings. However, I could tell by this time that London Live was getting a lot of bad press, and not only was it starting to concern me, but it was starting to concern others too. I kept my calm and trusted the process. I kept my mind focused on other things, I even produced, wrote, and directed a short film called 'Perceptions' *(you can find this on YouTube, type in: Film Perceptions St Raphs Estate, or if you are reading an ebook click here).* During these times of uncertainty, I was thinking about my income and my flat, at this stage I only had money from the acquisition and nothing coming in, I literally had the dice rolling on the acquisition of the next series and was starting to get anxious.

My phone pinged. It was an email from my agent with a request from the Bush Live Theatre to speak at an event, as they saw Mckenzies on London Live and wanted me to do a talk about underrepresented stories and perspectives. They were putting on a Barbadian family play of which I was invited to watch. I emailed my agency back and said it was a great idea and if they could forward my details to them as I was interested. Sounds straight forward, doesn't it? Did you find anything wrong with this? I didn't. Twenty minutes later after I responded I get this email from the agency.

Dear Samuell

Having spoken with the team just now we have decided to terminate our contract with you. This means that you will be free to negotiate and handle all projects directly. We will inform your US representatives of this,so you can deal with them directly. I will also let Amy liaise with you directly

We wish you all the best

I'm sure you are thinking 'what the hell?' I was! I wanted an answer, this agency represented me for 4 years and I had work through them! I wanted an answer as to why they were dropping me after 4 years. The response I got was a one liner...

Dear Samuell

I just feel we have reached a crossroad. As I said I wish you nothing but the futures best.

So, now I just lost my agent, with no proper explanation as to specifics! This was cold. The only thing I could do was come up with my own conclusions. I thought maybe they didn't like my independent movements, after all they didn't get any money from me for the McKenzies as it had nothing to do with them.

My perspective on that can be summed up with this question, "did they not think that the rise of my show would lead to a rise of them too"? There was no way of finding that out now as they had dropped me. So, I wasn't working, had no agent, and I was awaiting a response from London Live.

For all the practical people reading this you would probably say if you were me you would have a normal job in the meantime. This is true to a degree, BUT if you had gone through what I had gone through being in a normal job, you wouldn't be the same and it would have been hard, read soul killing, knowing that you tasted success and went backwards to the old usual routine. Two weeks went by and I decided to chase up on London Live after an article I saw online stating that they were going to have to cut down on local content. This was the response I got:

> Hi Samuel
>
> I'm well thanks, and yourself?
>
> As you know we've been considering AATM as part of our 2nd wave of acquisitions across all distributors, with ROI analysed against potential erformance. We're big fans of the show and the 2nd series is great, but unfortunately I'm now in a position to update you we will not be choosing to acquire it at this stage for London Live. Therefore, as per contractual agreement you're free to market this elsewhere.
>
> With best wishes,

I was gutted... I knew what this meant... I had to leave the flat and return home back to my parent's house. There was no way I was going to stay in the flat at the rate I was paying monthly, and not have any income. I chose that specific flat with the full faith that London Live would acquire the 3rd series. What now was I to do with the episodes I filmed a few months before? I felt like I had let my cast down and I was crushed. After EVERYTHING I had been through to get to this point, there was a block. It was like the universe only wanted to tease me but not give me what I wanted. I had sacrificed a lot to get to this point. Embarrassingly, I moved back into the family home and sharing a box room with my little brother.

I kept myself in the room and didn't want to leave. It was weird moving from a queen size bed to a single bed. The trampoline, I gave away to the children who lived next door where I was staying at the flat, they were happy. At least they were. I had never felt so clueless, numb, and speechless.

Have you the reader ever felt like you had so much talent, but no one really gave a shit even after you proved yourself? Even after you challenged the status quo? Even after you managed to get on TV with no film school experience? It's like I felt invisible. I knew my show was hot and I knew people loved it and wanted more! It was like there was this bridge that wasn't accessible or it always came down to someone else to decide whether you were good enough. I NEVER EVER doubted my talent and skill up to date. I didn't know what else to do, and like the agent said in the email, I guess I too was at crossroads.

This felt like a trip down memory lane of past failures - I was angry, upset and confused. I reached out to other networks and shared the information that 'All About the Mckenzies' was shown on TV, maybe that would help in terms of a consideration of the show being on another Network. I reached out to BBC, Channel 4, even the Africa channel. No responses. What was I to do? I had series 3 on a DVD and nothing was being done with it. I kept telling myself that I did not want to put it on YouTube, I wanted to feel like the show was moving forward not backward.

Months went by and I discovered an advert in an email newsletter. It was to do with a Broadcast Commissioning forum. This is an event that is held every year at a venue whereby commissioners from different networks, speak on various panels to an audience of producers and production companies telling them what's going on in TV and what they are seeking to commission. As I didn't know what else to do with my show, I thought there would be no harm in attending.

I didn't know what to expect from an event like this as I had never been to one before, surprisingly enough events like this did not attract youth and it didn't attract any web series content creators... I was the only one in this bracket that showed up, everyone else was a lot older than me. I had a few Mckenzie DVD's on me because you never know who you are going to meet, I was prepared. Sitting in the auditorium and probably the most inexperienced person in the room, I looked around me and saw many top-level producers that have seasoned credits on TV, here I was with my little show by going down an unconventional route as a hopeful.

The one panel that sparked my interest was a panel that was going to have the BBC1 controller Charlotte Moore being interviewed. *Reader, please bear in mind that these were times when the complaints about lack of diversity was on the rise.* As Charlotte spoke, everything she had mentioned in terms of what the BBC was looking for, I had in my pocket. She mentioned diversity, I ticked that boxed! She mentioned a family show, I ticked that box! She mentioned introducing new talent, I ticked that box! In a nut shell, I ticked all the boxes of what the BBC was looking for. It came to a point where the interviewer allowed the audience to ask questions and I remember my heart was pumping, like it wanted to get out of my chest and on the stage where Charlotte was! I immediately raised my hand, heart racing and nerves all over the place, I knew I had to say something, here goes: *"Hi Charlotte, thank you for giving your words of Wisdom. I have heard everything you have said in terms of what the BBC are looking for, I have a show which is of a family nature and it's about a British black family, something you've not had on your screens since 2005, its already filmed and made.*

Since that's something you have stated you are looking for and it ticks the box of everything you have asked, would you be open to looking at the idea if I give you a DVD right now?"

The room went silent, my heart slowed down. Immediately I thought to myself *"shit what did you just do?"* Lo and behold she agreed, and I was happy, I even got a round of applause for having the balls to *apparently* pitch to a BBC1 Controller. I didn't even know that what I did was a pitch, all I was did was speak from the heart with a desire for my lengthy period of blood, sweat and tears worth of work to be considered. Strangely enough a few other people wanted to know who I was at the event and were asking for DVD's off me which I gladly gave. Who would have thought that one action would have led to this? I even bumped into some people from Sky after the event had finished and gave them my DVD's.

After going home, I felt like it was a job well done and worth me going to the event. The question I was more interested in was what was to come from it. A couple of weeks went by and Charlotte emailed me back after I had followed up with her. This was her response:

Dear Samuel,

Sorry I've been away on holiday since I met you at the forum and only just had time to watch the DVD and catch up on emails. I enjoyed ep one. Some great characters and comedy moments. I'm afraid it doesn't feel like broad and mainstream enough for BBCOne, but I'd love to know more about how it came about. Is it a series commissioned and produced for London Live? If you could let me know more I'll try and hook you up with the right people at this end to discuss new comedy ideas.

Best

Charlotte

It was great that I got a response, and fair enough it wasn't broad and mainstream enough for BBC1. However, what happened next was Charlotte emailed the BBC3 comedy commissioner, which led to a meeting. I met with the commissioner who had since watched some private links I had sent him through email conversations. He had concerns with the show in terms of its development. He was also shocked that I made the show on such a small budget. He even stated what I had made was equivalent to £400,000 in terms of its quality! That was shocking to hear.

It really showed me that it always comes down to the 'talent' to make something happen. If 'talent' can make a small budget be perceived as higher budgets, then the focus should be on the 'talent' to get things done, and working with new talent. *I just want the reader to think about something for a moment. I had just proved to a commissioner and controller of a channel, that there was a 'capability' on my behalf to get the job done on a smaller budget, which could save a company money.*

The commissioner basically said that the show wasn't right for BBC3. Once again, I was annoyed because Charlotte said it was perfect for BBC3! The commissioner said that he would introduce me to other production companies, which he did.

Pic taken at 'Prove You Exist' event - 2013

I felt like a rat in a maze, going from one person to another, meeting to another meeting, and nothing came from it! It kind of felt like a humiliating game, all dependent on somebody else's 'perception' of what 'they' thought was good enough.

Something clicked for me, an epiphany, everyone had something different to say and it honestly felt like slavery. I felt like I was a slave going to the slave master for handouts and recognition. It also made me realise why so many people chose the web route. I was starting to feel like British TV was not a home for black family shows.

You, the reader, may think that this is a bit harsh, but everybody I was dealing with in meetings, was white. It's understandable to not understand a black perspective or black family show. I didn't know what else to do, so I ended up uploading series 3 to YouTube for everyone to view as I didn't want the show collecting dust. This was a very tiring journey and I had gone too far to give up, but it was just, I didn't know what else to do. I had been to many other TV events since the forum and even spoke on panels for many diversity debates. I even travelled to Birmingham and Leeds with the programme makers of the Barbadian family show 'Keeping up with the Joneses', we had screenings in these cities and spoke on panels at those events. It was regarding Caribbean invisibility. I also managed to get a talk at the Apple Store in Oxford Street in London. After the all promotion, only 5 people turned up and I knew 4 of them! This was very embarrassing and heart-breaking because there was no support from webseries creators and no support from the black community *(the very people that complain there's no black people on TV screens!)*

Apple store Regent Street

Barbados

Sun, cocktails and flying fish were calling me from Barbados to get away from everything. I flew out there and spent a week to realign myself. I had no plan, nothing, I just needed to think. In my hotel room the whole journey was spinning around my head, the ups, the downs, the teases of success and the let downs of failure. The one thing I truly appreciated the most was who I had become out of this process so far. I literally pushed myself to the max to be seen and disrupt what I call a zombie British TV industry. I tried my best not to entertain the thought that this was the end of the road.

Rommel Hall, myself and Chantelle S Evelyn- Birmingham

Whilst being in Barbados, I met up with the guys from 'Keeping up with the Joneses'. I was invited to one of their rehearsals and watched the actors in action. Months had gone by since I saw these guys in Birmingham, I was grateful I had someone's contact in Barbados as I knew no one. After having a conversation with Rommel, he suggested that I speak to the CBC (Caribbean Broadcasting Corporation) whilst I was there. I thought It was a good idea considering I didn't know what else to do, maybe the door in was through the Caribbean?

I researched where it was and made my way to the CBC. I will never forget the bus service in Barbados! It was small and ram packed and they blaze out music! It was very uncomfortable and I was literally pushed up against a big fat woman with an attitude. Funny now that I think about it, but at the time it was not funny!

Here I was, sitting in this small van with my Ipad and Mckenzies DVD and there was no plan, just simply me rocking up to the CBC to hand in a DVD hoping to speak to a commissioner or head of the network. I was told by Rommel that people were quite easy going at the Network and the fact that I was from Britain might spark some interest. I didn't know that I was going to be doing this before I left London, but there was no harm in making the most of my stay.

Selfie taken outside the CBC, Barbados 2014

I arrived and spoke to the receptionist. Unfortunately, the person I required was not around. I was told that I could leave the DVD in the pigeon hole of the person I needed. The receptionist also kindly gave me the number for the director of CBC, Rosemary Alleyene. I made the call but couldn't get through so I thought I'd try again when I was back in London as I was leaving the next day.

There I was back to London, fresh and calm thinking about my life and what to do considering everything that happened before I left. I didn't manage to speak to Rosemary as the number wasn't working; the only thing that worked was emails. Put it this way, the last email I got back from Rosemary was that she tried looking at the DVD and was going to get back to me the next day. That next day came and I never heard anything back, this went on for about another week. I then thought that it was *'another'* situation of *'no-go zone'*.

At this point I was even thinking about getting a normal job, but, how could I? Knowing that deep down there was this human yearning for more life and more expression. This person who wanted to challenge the status quo, this person that wanted more out of his life than spend his life force working for somebody else's dream. Gosh, all I wanted to do was 'act'! I never expected to create a show, write, produce and direct! Remember I was looking for those roles originally, but looking back I was forced to take on those roles due to the circumstances at the time. I'm glad I did, I ended up falling in love with those other roles as it brought more of *'me'* to the surface.

Was this whole journey meant to be for me to be developed as those roles, for something to come later down the line? Was I meant to be an invisible entity because I wasn't ready to be seen by the whole world? When embarking upon a journey of the unknown that's exactly what it is - unknown, which is why so many people do not even take the first step.

You, the reader, are aware of this roller coaster journey, you may even be thinking of similar roller coasters in your own life. There are many times you will feel you want to jump off the ride because you get sick, you throw up, you get dizzy, your shoe flies off, someone else throws up on you, the loop is too big, there are multiple loops at one time, the ride is too slow, the ride is too fast, there are many reasons that will make you want to get off the ride. But if you do, how would you know if your idea had worked? I say this because although I was still on the ride, I wasn't aware of the two massive loops coming in the distance.

Adrian

December 21st 2014, I get a Facebook message from a relative of Adrian, my cast member, and it said that I needed to call her urgently. I was trying to figure out what this was about, I laughed and thought he'd been arrested again for something stupid. No. Adrian was dead. The previous night he committed suicide by throwing himself on a train track. Blackout. I was numb, speechless, a train of a thousand pictures of experiences with Adrian flashed before my eyes. I couldn't believe it, it was a few days before Christmas! I was so shocked, I never thought anything of this nature would have happened to him. I hadn't spoken to Adrian since we had filmed earlier in the year. After I got off the phone, I sat down in the chair and for what seemed like a lifetime, I didn't move. I had to let the cast know, after a couple of days I put a message in the show WhatsApp group, the responses were what I expected. Everyone was shocked and very upset by the news, reactions were the same as we all thought of Adrian to be a very happy guy who enjoyed his acting, no one knew why he had done such a thing. My heart was unsettled and I wanted answers but how was I to get answers from him, he was dead.

With a cast member lost, I literally thought that the show was cursed. Every attack possible was being executed, it was as if all weapons used against me was doing their best to take me down. It was starting to win, as I slowly felt myself being pierced. I went to the funeral the next month and made a video tribute to Adrian. It was sad looking his 10yr old son in the eyes and telling him he needed to be strong for his family. The only support I could receive on the day was from Niaz, Fenella and Sarah the makeup artist. Everybody else couldn't attend the funeral for various reasons, but the good thing is they contributed towards the video tribute by recording messages each. It was time to go the graveyard and it was painful seeing that coffin lower into the ground. I took the shovel and did my bit in burying him, the last time I was at a funeral was at my grandmothers when I was like 10yrs old or something like that, I can't remember the age exactly. That was the day I said goodbye to a long-time friend and cast member.

Now that the funeral was over, what was I to do with everything? Changing the Ian character would not be easy. As it stood, I had series 3 on YouTube and no leads as to the next move. What was predominantly in my face at the time was the number of black actors that were flying off to the states and getting the recognition they deserved. Stories with Idris Elba, David Harewood, Naomi Harris etc., it seemed like a trend, a wave of Black British talent flying over to the States, because in the UK they were underrepresented and clearly not on screen! Anything that was being made was all YouTube and nothing mainstream, this was not what I wanted at all. I weighed up everything; the meetings that led nowhere, London Live, the agent dropping me, losing my flat, Adrian dying, the black actors off to the US, what should I do? Was the States the next avenue?

To check out the third series of All About The McKenzies, type in YouTube: All About The Mckenzies series 3, or if you are reading an ebook click here.

CHAPTER 6

LONDON TO LA

I made the decision that I was going to LA; I was done with the UK. Everything was proving not to work out for me as I'm sure you can understand from reading my story so far. I spoke with my parents and they understood, so they were going to give me a budget of money to get me started. My responsibility was for how that money was going to be used and for me to get a job whilst I was out there. This decision was made at midnight new year's going into 2015, and there was no going back from this decision as I booked my flight there and then. I got my O1 Visa sorted *(this is an entertainment visa that allows you to work in entertainment in the States).*

The date for me to leave was the 8th April 2015. I shared my departure on Facebook and funnily enough, I had the most 'likes' on that post than any other in the history of me being on that site.

Selfie at Heathrow Airport April 2015

I had literally been through a lot! It seemed that there was no answer in Britain, but there were answers in the States, and I was willing to find out where I fitted in. This was the second of the giant loops in the roller coaster ride, Adrian had been the first giant loop. I already had a networking week planned with various agents, managers, casting directors etc. all through a service called 'Industry Hollywood' led by Richard Burke, a former actor *(You can find more details about this service on http://industryhollywood.com/)*

After arriving in LA, my first stop was staying temporarily in a hostel until I found a place to stay for rent. I stayed in a place called Banana Bungalows, which was located on Hollywood Boulevard. I hated it from the moment I walked in. My first impression was that of a university party as there was a lot of loud music and alcohol. Banana Bungalows is kind of like a Backpackers place where lots of international people stay for a short period. I was staying in a room with 3 other people comprised of bunk beds. Talk about being uncomfortable. I was later to discover that this place was filled with bed bugs!

Luckily, my bed didn't have any but there were various cases of others having that issue! Prior to leaving London I had been on a Skype call with someone called Kandace, who was referred to me by one of my friends in London.

Kandace was from London but now lives in LA, and she was a great connection to have out there as she showed me quite a lot about where things were, getting my social security number, my bank account, and you are yet to find out that Kandace saved me in terms of accommodation, because the place I originally wanted to rent out had major problems with the tenants and furniture. I was only staying at Banana Bungalows for 2 weeks so I had to stick it out until my next accommodation was sorted.

The networking week was starting and I met up with about 12 other actors and Richard. The schedule was packed for the week. I kept 'All About The McKenzies' out of my head whilst I was doing this networking week, and decided to focus on my acting for this period. I was required to learn two monologues for my meetings. *I won't go into so much detail about the networking week her.* To cut a long story short, this was where I got my manager who still represents me today. Throughout the week, I met different people in the industry, including immigration lawyers who deal with visas. It was a fun week, and this was the second networking week I had done, as the first one I did was in 2010. I shall discuss this more in the later chapter.

I had a couple of friends reach out to me, one of whom was a director I met at the HBFF 2011, and another director I met at the LA Webfest 2012. They knew I was in town and one of them wanted to offer me a short film gig, and the other a play. I was happy! No audition needed! An actor's dream! This was literally within the same month that I had arrived, so talk about a fast turnaround! I won't delve too much into this though, but the days were fun doing these projects, they were each a one day gig and I really enjoyed it

What was important, do you remember when I said Kandace saved me for accommodation? The place where I wanted to go, I found out when I got there that there was no bed in the room and there were no lights! Where was I supposed to sleep? This was not on and was not what was agreed when I said I'd move in. I had turned up there late in the night with all my stuff only to then find out this info. I called Kandace, explained the situation, and she called in a favour with someone that she used to live with called Cassandra to enquire about her spare room. The beauty about moving in there was that I would be in the same apartment block as Kandace as she was only down the corridor. The jacuzzi and swimming pool was a bonus feature too. I moved into Cassandra's, but realised this woman had a hoarding disorder. She had items all over the place - it was a mess! I didn't know how she managed to survive in such a dump. I had to arrange my room in a way where I had to remove her stuff and throw into the ocean of madness with her belongings. The safest place to walk was in my room!

After the room was cleaned and in a position of 'basic' living, I could start to think about my life and it leading to this moment. I told the cast from the show that I had settled in; I was aware that they wanted to know what was going on with the show. I wish I had an answer to give them because as you have witnessed through these pages, I didn't have any answers, I just kept moving forward and taking the opportunities that I saw that were linked to my show. I went for a walk, but LA is a place where you need a car! It is massive! Uber was my best friend whilst staying out there. I even learned to use the metro system underground and some buses. Whilst on my walk I was approached by a guy who was asking me for directions, I think he must have heard from my accent that I wasn't from around there. We got into a conversation and he told me about TSAW (Tasha Smith Acting Workshop). As soon as he mentioned this to me, I immediately thought back to 2011 when my pilot was stolen, my friend Pauline called me explaining that she got back from Philly participating in a Tasha Smith Acting workshop. I thought this was a clue from the universe so I looked further into these workshops when I got home.

I checked on the website and it said that Monday nights were free for the public to audit the class that Tasha was teaching. For those who don't know, Tasha Smith is a phenomenal actress that has starred in many projects, *Tyler Perry's Daddy's Little Girls, For better or for worse, Why did I get married? Why did I get married too? Empire, just to name a few.* She is also a teacher of the Chubbuck technique from acting coach Ivana Chubbuck *(I personally have done two masterclasses with Ivana and she is great!)* When I attended the class I was blown away by some of the students and the way I saw Tasha teach was like no other; She brought spirituality into teaching and it was powerful, I could now understand what my friend Pauline was talking about years ago. I met Tasha in person and she is fantastic! I said that I wanted to join and do classes once a week and through doing these classes I met some good friends,

Queanna, Gary, Chance, Elle, and a few others. The aim is not to talk about these classes in depth, I mention this to you to show you what I was doing whilst I was out there and how it led to a screening of the McKenzies in the Chinese theatre in Hollywood, *more about this later*. I forgot to tell you, before I left for LA, I submitted 'All About The McKenzies' into the ABFF 2015 (American Black Film Festival). This was a festival to be happening in May 2015 and the show was selected for screening! I was on my way to NYC!

I was going to be staying with cousin Whitney, whom I had never physically met before. She had an apartment in Manhattan and I was to be there for a few days alone as she was going on a trip to Cuba. Facebook is great - you meet family you never knew existed. Also, whilst being out there, I met more family and discovered that they had their own funeral home called 'Benta's funeral Homes'. There's a lot more to the Benta name than I thought, no one else in my family knew of these Benta's!

I experienced the train system in New York. I had never been on one of these before; I had only seen them in movies where there was a chase, or someone got brutally murdered or there was a fight. I was in my Maroon suit heading to the festival and I was squeezed up in the train next to New Yorker strangers. *Reader, I was excited, but I was also scared as this was a path unknown and I was by myself.* I had a tariff on my phone which allowed me to call home for free and at various times, so I would call my family and check in on them. They were more interested in what was happening with me, which was understandable.

JaNeika James, myself and JaSheika James (Writers of Empire)

I got to the festival and it was going to be a couple of days of screenings and panels. One particular panel I was interested in was the 'The Empire Writers', they were going to be interviewed and I was intrigued to know what the writersooms were like, and I was proud to see that it was majority black writers, *something unheard of in the UK TV industry!* I managed to get a conversation with two of the writers, twin sisters JaSheika and JaNeika James, they knew I was from London by my accent and they wanted to know how Empire was doing in the UK, at that time season one of Empire had just been acquired by E4 and was halfway through the season. I spoke to them about Britain, diversity, not a lot of black people on screen and that what I was doing with my show. They were shocked with what I was telling them about the TV industry over in Britain. They thought *they* had a diversity problem but when they heard *my* perspective, they were at ease and very appreciative for what they had. I grabbed a quick picture with them and got some inside scoop into series 2 of Empire before everyone else.

Sarah, myself and Aniya

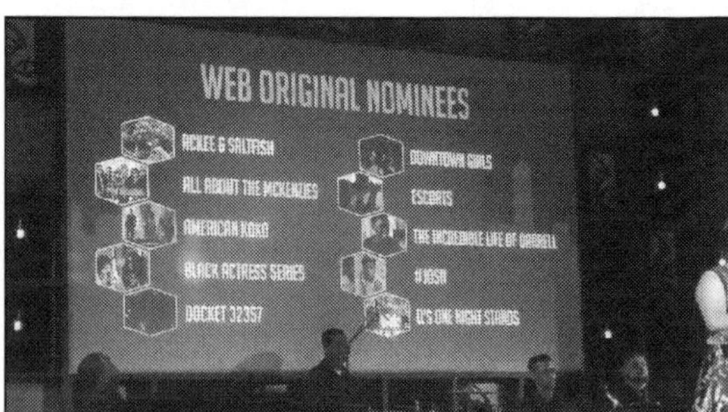

ABFF 2015 - NYC

I was proud walking around the festival and seeing so many people of colour being celebrated for their shows and films, there was more of an *'acceptance'* over here than what I had ever experienced in London, and what I was *'learning'*, was that there was a major different *'attitude'* toward work and success. The *'culture'* over here was *'let's go do it!'* whereas Britain is more restricted, conservative - work alone, and if I was to compare with the Americans... *lazy!* Did you feel offended? That wasn't my intention but I stand by what I said. There is a *'reason'* why Americans are a lot more further ahead in success, business, and scope of this industry. I mean *come on*, they dominate our TV screens and movie theatres! They have a different *'mindset'*. *I will talk more about this in the other half of this book.*

All About The Mckenzies was going to be screened with many other series in a cinema in Times Square. As I looked at the line up I saw another black British web series 'Ackee and Saltfish' which was also going to be screened. I was happy as I knew one of the actresses in that from drama workshops I attended years ago. Sarah the makeup artist from my show was in NYC because she was visiting Aniya who now lived there, and it warmed my heart that both ladies supported me whilst I was there at the screening. They came down and surprised me! It felt like a Mckenzie reunion but only with a couple of people. The theatre was half packed and I was buzzing, when Mckenzies screened I sat there proud and had a few laughs from the Americans. I didn't know how they were going to take my show originally but they really seemed to like it. I remember sitting there thinking my show could do so well over here that it gave me ideas to start researching when I got back to LA.

I got to mingle with other web series content creators and had more people to hang with whilst at the festival. One in particular was an actress, *Angela Lewis,* who created the web series 'Black Actress', we got on quite well, she lived in NYC and was going to be heading to LA soon, as she was planning an event out there. I made sure we had each other's details as you never knew where this could lead. Remember Tasha Smith? She was holding her actor's workshop at this festival too, and she had a premiere of her short film *'Boxed In',* that she wrote and directed. I thought it would be nice to support her so I made sure it was a priority for me to attend. The auditorium was packed, a full house, well done, Tasha! She knew how to work a room with that powerful, passionate voice of hers when she made her entrance! What really struck me was when she recognised who I was from her classes in LA, and she asked me to sit with her crew at the front, I felt privileged. Here I was, a guy from London who admired this woman from films I'd seen her in, and now I was sitting with her in a screening for her film! Madness! The film was great and I was happy to support her; it was about a black man in NYC with bipolar disorder. She had magnificent reviews and it was well deserved.

ABFF 2015 Brochure

It was coming up to the end of the festival and thus the end of NYC for me, what an experience! Not only had I met family, I understood more about them, their background and history, I looked after my cousin's lazy dog! I know I didn't mention much of this but I merely wanted to focus on the 'necessary' elements of this journey!

I was surprised by two of my crew members from the Mckenzies supporting me, I even managed to get a self-tape done for an audition, it was for Brandy's show which was on BET. I never got the part for it but was appreciative that I was seen for it. The beauty of my manager was that she went all out to find me a place to record my self-tape in NYC.

Back in LA! I was pumped, I dedicated some time to research the different Networks and how I could get my show in there somehow. Online it was tough to find contacts! Not that I was surprised, of course, as I can imagine the amount of people that want their shows on TV and hound these networks. I even went to the extreme of researching how I could get the show as part of in-flight entertainment for aeroplanes.

I had spent all day researching and contacting different airlines all of which led to nowhere in the end. Man, why was it so tough to get the show out there? What was I missing? This road that was never-ending was getting me down, so I thought writing would keep me on a balanced level and feeling good.

One day I sent a WhatsApp message to the Mckenzie cast, and was asking for their input. Everyone was throwing in their ideas and then it dawned on me, why write a series when I could write a film? I made this my focus, I set a goal and said that in 3 weeks' time I would have a feature film written for the show.

Money was starting to run low and I was seeking a server job. I wanted to be smart about this, so I handed in my CV to a restaurant in Universal City, Bubba Gumps. I applied there because it was right next to Universal studios and many of their staff ate at Bubba Gumps. I ended up getting the job and experienced what it was like to be a server. I absolutely hated having to memorise a menu, it was an arduous task, but it had to be done as I had bills to pay, and the original budget I came to LA with was starting to dry up. Serving tables was great, my accent paid off and I got tipped for every table I served. I remember saving all my tips and I had saved about $600! This could cover my rent for a month; however, every shift was different and the tips varied, some low, some high. I'm aware that there is now a Bubba Gumps in Leicester Square, for those who don't know of this restaurant, walk in, and have a look, you'd see where I was working in LA.

Now that I had a job sorted, I wanted to manage my time when I wasn't working to make sure that I was getting my script for the film written. My schedule was set where, before work if I was doing an evening shift, I would dedicate the mornings to writing, and obviously, days I wasn't working I would also write my script.

Simultaneously whilst grinding in LA, I was getting A LOT of auditions. There were so many that my manager was shooting my way that I couldn't keep up. Don't get it twisted, I was grateful! It was just whoa... I had to manage working, auditions, self-tapes, and write a script. In London, I never received this many auditions because there wasn't that much work for black actors in TV - in America there is SO MUCH! There were more opportunities for work here. However, there was more competition because there were more actors. I must say this, coming to LA was a huge shock to my system because of the fast-paced work ethic and culture, something I had never got from London; it was like having to readjust and developing new brain cells to deal with a different 'energy'. My manager ended up getting me a meeting with an agency out here and I got representation. Now I had a manager and an agency, it felt brilliant because I knew of many hopefuls of American actors who struggle to even get representation. I guess you must count your blessings.

Starbucks on Sunset/LaBrea was a regular spot for me to write. I'd get out my laptop and order a large coffee and get to work. Sometimes I would be in there long hours. Three weeks went by and I managed to complete my script. Not bad, but I think my motivation came from wanting to experience a different reality other than being a server, getting this script written was a necessity. I turned the film into a sci-comedy where the McKenzies went to space and Granddad was on a mission to save planet earth. I have a crazy imagination what can I say? As I was writing it, my thoughts about Adrian came to my mind and I had to hold myself together. This film was to involve CGI and special effects, something I had no experience of.

One day I took a trip to LA film school and managed to get myself in past security to find a department that dealt with that type of stuff. After doing some investigating I found a guy who did some work on the Hunger Games films, and he advised me what was needed. I admit I was a bit overwhelmed as it was a major stretch from everything I had done before, either way I didn't care because I was all about growth and learning.

Advert for Mckenzies screening in Hollywood

Later that week I received an email from Andrea Lewis, do you remember that webseries creator I met in NYC? She was in LA with her producer and we arranged a meeting. There's a restaurant off Hollywood/Caheunga Blvd called Kitchen 24 where we agreed to meet.

I'd been to this place a few times, they are open 24 hours and serve the most amazing chicken sandwich... anyways, after getting to know each other a bit more, Andrea brought me in on a show she was looking to create, it was called 'Married', she wanted me to play the husband. A British guy who got married to an American girl who were newlywed. After reviewing the scripts, I was up for it! After all, I needed some good news and it would be great to be acting again whilst I was figuring out what to do with the McKenzies film. She said she was looking to film it sometime in October over a weekend.

This all sounded fine to me and we decided to keep in touch and meet up another day when her actress friend was available so we could all do lunch. As I was leaving she told me about her event that was coming up in September which was being held at Russell Simmon's All Def Digital building, from what I recall, it was about black actresses and content creation, and there was going to be a panel of guests. I said to Andrea that I'd definitely attend to support her. *Do you see that reader? Networking is so key because you never know where those connections will come in handy, I met this person in NYC!*

Fast forward on a Monday night, I was at TSAW for class. The evening was powerful as usual, I witnessed acting techniques and warm ups that I'd never seen before. One that I love with what Tasha does is where she gathers the group together and does what she calls, an *emotional dump*. This is where each actor must literally dump all their emotions about someone who has caused them pain in their life. They would have to picture that person and speak aloud like it was that them they were talking to. This can be quite uncomfortable but also very empowering for the actors. The stuff I witnessed and heard was very emotional and heart felt, at times I wanted to cry after hearing the content that came out of some of these actor's mouths with what they been through.

My love for acting grew at that moment because it reminded me how gifted we all are, and that all our pain was for a purpose. I could certainly testify to that! Sitting in the audience was a guy called Dave Brown. He was a friend of Tasha and at the end of class he promoted his film festival called 'Indie Night Film Festival'. This is an event that happens every Saturday at the Chinese Theatre in Hollywood *(10 minutes from where I lived),* the festival showcased filmmaker's work and was also an opportunity for networking. Big names were known to be invited to these screenings, names such as: Robi Reed, John Singleton, Twinkie Byrd, Tisha Campbell Martin and many more. As soon as Dave promoted his event, I immediately thought *"let's get a screening of the McKenzies in Hollywood*!". I made a note of his festival's details and the next day I submitted for it. *For those of you who want to know more about Dave's festival and/or if you are interested in screening your stuff in Hollywood, check out his website.*

I spoke with Dave on the phone - Mckenzies was a go! I was about to have a screening of my show at the same place where they screen some of Hollywood's premieres for big blockbuster movies! This was a big deal for me. After experiencing ABFF in NYC, who knew what was to come from this screening at the Chinese Theatre. I made sure I invited everyone that I had met since I got to LA, including Tasha. The episode that I chose to be screened was series 3, episode 1, which starred Adrian. I wanted him to get a spotlight and show him my respects now that he was no longer with us. Invites weren't promising as most people were unavailable; I was beginning to think if I'd even have an audience.

From what I knew there was going to be a screening for about 5 shows that night. I had a few people saying they would attend and I had a few people drop out. In total, I had about 3 people that turned up, Tasha couldn't make it because she was in Chicago filming series 2 of Empire. One person from TSAW made it and a couple of people I met whilst on the journey in LA. It wasn't much, but at least it was me not being by myself. The event was free but everyone that attended had to buy a minimum of two drinks. The theatre was half full and there was a guest celebrity who attended, actor Morris Chestnut. He was promoting a new show he was in called *Rosewood,* which was soon to be coming out. I had the privilege of meeting this man, once again it was an actor I've admired from seeing him in movies, and he was there to view the shows that were to be screened, including mine.

Myself and Actor Morris Chestnut

Its times like these you wish you had your friends and family; this was my second screening since I'd left London. Deep within me I kept asking myself *"what's to come from this, what's to come from this?"*. The control freak in me wanted to know what was the next step before the event had even finished. *Get it together Sam!* It was that time, my show was starting. The title sequence was on the big screen, this was the biggest screen I had ever seen my face on! I lowered myself a little in my seat and was at the back with my supporters, mainly so I could see reactions from people in the audience so I would know what worked and didn't worked. I wanted to know which bits they found funny and which bits I thought were funny that they didn't. This is important to know because up to this stage I was the only one greenlighting my show.

Viewing Adrian on the screen knowing he was gone was tough. If only he were alive to see himself right now, he would have been proud. I was proud of him. I was proud for the whole team of Mckenzies because I knew how much we had grown from where we started. The show was over and good feedback once again, I had an opportunity to walk on the stage and have a quick interview in front of everybody. *Was there someone in this audience that was going to be the next piece of my puzzle?* These were the types of questions that were flying around my head as I walked up to the stage and grabbed the microphone.

When asked the question about why I was in Hollywood in the first place, my response was so passionate that it touched people. Truth be told what I wanted was for the TV industry in Britain to be more open to people of colour being on screen in a positive light. They were very quick to acquire black American content like *Empire* and *Fresh Prince,* but what about their own people? What about the British led productions for black people as a main cast? This set me on fire because it hurt knowing that I went out of my way to be the change I wanted to see, only to taste a bit of success and then be pushed aside. I had felt so rejected and unappreciated that I had to flee the country. This meant so much for me, my dreams and what I desired in life meant so much for me, that I literally left everything and everyone behind to pursue it. *Reader, going to America was not an easy decision to make; it was the same as me living in the ocean and treading water looking around for a lifeboat, where someone who saw the life in me would throw out a float to save me.*

There was a quick networking opportunity after the screening, and strangely enough not a lot of people hung around; I met a few of the filmmakers and that was pretty much it. I went to the bar to grab a glass of red wine and looked upon the few people that were there who I had spoken to, but where was the next piece of the puzzle?! What was I to do from this moment?? People were leaving and I stood by the bar clueless. *Don't get me wrong, reader, I was appreciative for this experience but I expected an action and reaction, not stuck in emotional limbo by the bar...* After arriving at home carefully watching my step through the overcrowded, not needed items of collections from Cassandra, I managed to survive the obstacle course getting to my room. I shut the door behind me and literally sat on the floor and was silent.

Have you the reader ever had those moments where you're at home by yourself, you sit down and are deep in thought? I had many of these whilst in LA. Coming out here was a massive step. I was away from family, my daughter, friends, and familiarity. Everything was so foreign, I even kept asking myself if I made the right decision. Many decisions were made during this whole story and to be honest all I ever knew was that there had to be some *'decision'* to be made.

In life, everything is a choice. We may not know if those choices we make are the correct ones, we just know that we will be presented with choices.

Many times, I wanted to go home, but what if this was the place to be? I love the hot weather and the fact it never really rains over here but, I felt invisible. In school, we are trained to always be *'logical* and *'practical'*, but from what

I was discovering about my journey was that I was leading an *'unconventional'* route, a route which cannot be taught in school because it is a unique path given to *'you'*. I think everyone wants to know the *easy way*, or the simple *5 step formula* for success. I witnessed this at many events I went to in LA and even in London! Everyone wants to know *'how'* to get to the top or the *'way in'*. The truth is, there is no *direct* way in. What I do know is that there is a hidden law that governs all things *(I will talk more about this in part 2).*

I'd never seen myself as a failure. It would be impossible for me to think that because I had already proven something to myself- I can do this! My self-confidence increased as I continued this whole journey, but that doesn't mean that the demons didn't rear their heads with doubts. I think what kept me strong throughout this process was personal development books and watching videos of inspirational speakers like Bob proctor, Rev Ike and Les Brown. In a society of negativity, where we are told we have no power, and seeing many celebrities on screen doing their thing and being successful whilst we sit there viewing them thinking to ourselves *'what about me?'*, sometimes we need words of inspiration and encouragement.

I truly believe that we all deserve to have what we want. There's a light inside each of us that deserves to be shone onto the world. Many things, rejections, hardships, and people can dim that light. How many people have quit on their dreams? How many people do you know who are just *'getting by'* and surviving? That seems to be where people's focus mainly goes, onto surviving. So much time is spent focussing on it that people tend to lose sight of where it is that they are going overall. All I had was my film script and my money was running low, truth be told, Bubba Gumps was not getting me by *enough* and I was soon going to have to decide about what I was going to do.

Myself and Actress Keesha Sharp

September came and Andrea's event was kicking off. We had met up a couple of times prior to this as I met with the actress I'd be playing alongside, it was a lady called *Iman Milner*. I arrived slightly late as I was stuck in the Uber because of traffic. It was a surreal experience walking into a building where Russell Simmons regularly works, he wasn't there unfortunately. Andrea packed out the room, I squeezed myself through the crowd who were standing at the back who couldn't get seats as they were taken up, and I looked at the panel, one of the guests was actress Keesha Sharp *(Girlfriends/Lethal Weapon/The People VS OJ Simpson).* I knew Keesha from Girlfriends as I used to watch it when I was younger, and ironically enough that show was one of the scripts I researched when starting off the McKenzies. I managed to speak to Keesha in the end and we had a conversation about a short film she had written and filmed. I also told her about my show and the recent screening. I could tell there was more convo to be explored here but the woman had so many fans that wanted to talk to her. We exchanged details and agreed to meet up at a later date.

I think it's important for me to mention at this point that I was doing my best to keep a happy face because what was on my mind was my rent for next month potentially not being paid. My shifts had been cut at restaurant and I wasn't making as much. When I say, I had to watch every dollar I used, I meant it! It was one of those moments where you knew there was a bomb ticking but you didn't know when it would explode. Keesha and I kept up via email and she watched my show online. She had forwarded me a couple of scripts she had written *(I won't mention the names of them for confidentiality).* We met up one day at a Starbucks at the farmer's market located near the Grove. We talked for about an hour. This woman was amazing and very ambitious. At the time I saw her, she hadn't done Lethal Weapon or The People's Story VS OJ Simpson, from what I recall she was still auditioning and mainly working on her own projects. I'm in the UK now and watching her on Lethal Weapon a year and a half later makes me so proud, because prior to all of that I met this woman in person and had a chat with her one on one in Starbucks! I remember she tried talking to me in a British accent and it was so funny. This meet up was us discussing our paths and how we got to where we were with what we had done, creativity, positivity, content creation, we even talked about potential collaborations in the future.

Anything is possible and the important thing to remember is everyone you meet is for a reason, it might not be known as to why you have met that person, but believe me when I say the answer will come later when you least expect it. I made sure I got a quick video with myself and her recording a message for you! *Little did I know that the purpose of creating that video was to be used later down the line for you who's reading the lines of this book*. Here it is, enjoy! Type in YouTube: *'Keesha Sharp and Samuell Benta.'* Or for the those reading this as ebook...

It was approaching 7 months since I had left London. Who was I kidding? I needed help! Guidance and even financial handouts! It was an embarrassing position to be in. So far, the list was this: I never received any roles I had auditioned for, my daughter was soon to be 6yrs old and I couldn't imagine not being there for her, the rent was due with Cassandra and I didn't have the full money, the novelty of being a server had worn off and I wanted to leave the restaurant, my fridge was empty, nothing came from my screening, and my bank balance was only enough to barely pay the rent or I had another decision... book a flight back home. I couldn't ask for any more money from my parents as they had given me a lot already. The server job wasn't cutting it for me and the travel fare back and forth to work was draining me. I needed a miracle or I was being faced with having to go home, which that idea didn't seem so bad due to the circumstances. The problem with that though is I would miss the opportunity to be in Andrea's Married web series. Decisions, decisions!

The date approached for rent and I had the money, but that's ALL the money I had, there was no food in the fridge and I had a few dollars in my wallet. It was October 2015 and my daughter's birthday was on the 21^{s} I was in a rut, a hole, and was potentially going to be on the streets of LA homeless. I did my best to avoid paying Cassandra her rent. I avoided her when she got home and I made sure I left the house before she woke up. She was so busy that even she nearly forgot to ask me for my rent. It was only when I got a call from Kandace that she said how Cassandra had called her and said I never paid her. An immediate decision had to be made. This was the one decision where I had to be logical and practical *(even though I hate these words).*

LA had been an amazing experience for me, I replayed a movie of all the experiences I had from arriving and being at the Banana Bungalows all the way up to meeting Keesha. A decision was made. I was booking a flight to London to leave the very same day. I felt bad about this because Cassandra wasn't getting her rent, but I was in survival mode and tips wasn't exactly perfect at the time where I was working. I packed my suitcase when Cassandra went out and I rounded up as much as I could take. I gave Kandace a call and gave her the heads up, she understood, and I saw her for the last time. I jumped into an UBER to head back to the airport with only a few dollars in my wallet. I had to hold out until I got back to London. *Thank the universe for food on the aeroplane as I didn't have enough for basics.* It was back to London for me, I had mixed emotions and weighed up the entire 7 months that I was out there. You, the reader, is soon to realise what the whole purpose of LA was really all about.

CHAPTER 7

THE SELF-MADE SHOWRUNNER

Back in London, I was welcomed by rain and cold as I stepped off the plane. The atmosphere hit me as I was so used to hot weather, the thing is, I loved it as familiarity hit me with *home sweet home*. As I carried my suitcase down the ramp all the way through the airport leading to the underground to catch the tube home, multiple thoughts were flying around my head, *'is this really happening? What am I to do now? I need a job! I have no agent here!'*. It felt weird. I felt like I had changed, as I looked at the public something wasn't *right*. I'm not the one to judge but everything felt so *slow* as I saw the British walking around. Even being on the tube again, there was a major difference in *energy*. I felt stagnation and a lot of fear emanating from people, it was a different vibe from being in LA all those months seeing a fast work paced, happier, open minded culture. Not to be so dramatic, but I felt like I was in another world and surrounded by zombies. Don't be offended if you are British reading this, I mean it when I say that there's a major difference in energy between

Brits and Americans. My brain had changed and I felt like a new person.

My family had moved into a new house and I discovered my new bed was either the couch or the floor due to there not being enough rooms. My parents weren't expecting me to back home, remember? My consequence of returning would mean that I was to not have my own room. At this point I didn't care as I was glad to be back and knew that in a few days I'd be going to see my daughter for her 6th birthday. When I managed to get a moment by myself, I reflected to look at what my options were from this point. I wasn't expecting to be back but here I was. My priority was to find some work as I needed money, so I reapplied to an old work place which was a call centre for actors called RSVP. It was the same job I had when I was writing series 1 of the McKenzies in 2012, the difference was, I was in a different department which was more *tolerable.* In other words, my job wasn't threatened on me making any sales over the phone. This job was to help me get back on my feet.

I messaged the cast and arranged a script readthrough for the McKenzies film, which I held at my mum's house; it was so fun and the script came to life! It was nice seeing the guys again; I hadn't seen most of them since we did series 3 and a lot had happened since then, Adrian's death, NYC, and LA. They were asking me questions as to when the film was going to be shot and how. I didn't have an answer. I had only just got back. I said the main point of doing the read through was to hear the words on the page and make sure that everything was in the right place, and a general catch up. During these times, I was receiving emails from my manager in LA as she wasn't aware that I was not coming back for a while, everything happened so fast that I wasn't even thinking about all that stuff, I had been in survival mode. I explained my situation to her and she understood saying that she would still put me up for auditions which I could self-tape over here.

In the first few months being back, I started doing talks at various different events in the personal development sector. It all started by me desiring to talk after attending a friend's event and seeing inspiring entrepreneurs. The main point with each of these speakers was a common thing that they all kept reiterating, *'what's your story?'* and *'what's your why?* Each of them had powerful stories of things that have happened in their lives which have led them to now do what they are doing. I knew my story so far with what I had overcome and challenges I had to deal with, I also knew why I was doing it and I wanted to share it with others. From that point I went out of my way to put myself forward for speaking gigs and the weirdest thing happened, all my talks were like a theatre performance mixed with engaging PowerPoint presentations. It was like 'acting' with a purpose to inspire and provoke thought.

Throughout the months, I was speaking at different events, ones which I put myself forward for and people were reaching out to me to speak at theirs too. I still do it to this day as I love giving back and I enjoy talking. My realization from all of this was that I wouldn't be speaking if I never had a story to tell and the McKenzies journey was a *story*! Had I not had experienced everything I went through I wouldn't have anything to say. I felt I had an obligation to free others and share knowledge and insight. I spoke at family events, entrepreneur events, students at universities, schools, and youth events, and as I felt a new string to my bow of talent, I felt that this whole new path was rewarding.

If I look back when this all started, it was due to dissatisfaction, and that dissatisfaction became a creative state that would eventually unlock the writer, director, producer, and speaker in me. Did I plan for this? No I never, but I can tell you this, it gave me a major self-confidence boost with a defined definiteness of purpose. I felt empowered and knew that I could do anything I put my mind to. I knew that what helped was all the personal development I had been doing throughout. My understanding of life, purpose and creating reality was beginning to all click.

I Am Potential, Event - 2016

Speak Now or Forever Hold Your Dreams Event – 2016

The call centre was starting to get to me, it was paying my bills but inwardly I was dying. Sitting at my cubicle I had a set of notes that I was jotting down, it was me figuring out what else I could do for money that could help me leave where I was. My immediate thought was production jobs, surely after producing 3 series of a show, that I'd be able to easily get producer/director freelance work or even production related jobs. I researched online and found a talent website for production opportunities. I created an account and sought out work for different companies. I had applied for many producer/director roles and even roles for creative agencies. My reel was updated for my profile so that I had a visual to show of my work, I was very confident with what I had, all there was now was for me to apply.

It was around June 2016, and I had sifted through so many job opportunities, I either got rejection emails or no response. I even went out my way to do follow up phone calls, all to which no avail. Why did I feel like I've been here before? Oh, yes, the networks! Laughing was my way of coping though the situation but this was serious, being at the call centre was not going to be for my lifetime! One evening I once again looked at my profile to see if there were ways I could improve it and then I noticed that there was a section that said 'testimonial', I needed to get some sort of testimony from someone who could recommend me but I didn't know who to pick as I had worked for myself. I had contacted the lady I met who introduced me to London Live but I had no response. I thought a bit deeper and then *'Patrick'* was the name that floated to my mind. Patrick used to run in-house production for the BBC, and I met him one time at the BAFTA building when Lenny Henry was doing a talk. This was around 2014. I hadn't worked with this guy before, but he had seen my movements online per what he told me. It made sense to ask him for a testimonial, and if I had it on my profile it may have helped me get work.

After sending him a Facebook message, he replied instantly and said that he would be happy to provide me with one. Then the weirdest thing happened, readers, he said to me that he was just about to contact me because, he had a meeting with the commissioner from ITV and wanted to talk to me about a potential production opportunity.

I was curious as to what this meant so I asked to meet up with him one day. BAFTA was the location for the meeting and when we sat down, I was wondering what this was all about. He told that ITV2 was looking for fresh talent to work with for their fresh season, which was to take place in November 2016. It would be a month of pilots from 4 different content creators leading after Black History Month. He said they wanted a new show idea and would that interest me. *You bet it would!*

I didn't want to get my hopes up so I said that I would get thinking of a show idea, but in the meantime, he should give my McKenzies DVD to the commissioner, so that he would see the quality of what I was capable of. We agreed and he said he'd contact me in two weeks' time. This was probably the biggest highlight I had received since I got back from LA. I was happy, all that was next was for me to start thinking of ideas for a new show, so I got straight to it.

Wasting no time, I got my ideas together and came up with a comedy regarding a couple and a talk show. I even went to the extent of writing the script and treatment. I knew I had to wait for two weeks because Patrick said he'd get back to me so I didn't stress about not getting any responses back before then. It took me 2 days to write a script for a pilot episode for this comedy and I thought that this would be perfect for ITV2.

My meditation retreat was the day after and it was for me to be away for 10 days in silence. *Reader? I had quit my call centre job as my life force was being depleted. By writing this script and anticipating ITV2, it brought me back to life and I couldn't bare being at that job anymore. No, you're right it wasn't practical but neither was the whole journey!*

After I got back from my retreat which was about two weeks, I never saw any messages from Pat. Patience was a virtue so I thought I'd give it a few more days and wait. I waited and waited and still no response; anxiety started to kick in, I then thought that this was another one of those things where it was a *'hype'* meeting and nothing happened from it. *It's kind of like when you go to a lot of networking events and you meet people who hand you their business cards, did you even see them again? Did they even contact you or did you contact them? That's what this felt like.* The practical side of me thought about looking for a normal job again, this was ridiculous! All this journey and for what?! A hype meeting?! Universe give me a frigging break!

Another two weeks went by. I woke up one morning and looked at my IPad screen. There was an email from Pat and it said, *"call me at 9am, I think I have some good news!".* What a great start to the morning! There was hope! I called him at 9am and he told me that the commissioner had been on holiday and seen my McKenzies DVD, the response was, with a bit of polish the show had legs. *Reader, I didn't think this was about McKenzies, I thought it was about a new show idea.* A fire had been reignited, did this mean that 'All About The McKenzies' was going to be on ITV2? I was excited, this was a major network! This wasn't a new start-up like London Live, I'd be reaching hundreds and thousands of people all over the country!

My brain felt like it was doing aerobics and breakdancing. One concern Pat had was if I'd be able to get the show done in such a short period. I told him that I had a whole series of 6x30minute episodes filmed in 13 days - what would doing a pilot be? Not to be cocky but this *young man* had experience, and was a self-starter, and had been training on the underground for a very long time. ITV didn't know who they were about to be dealing with!

A meeting was called for me and Patrick to meet with the commissioner at the ITV building in Waterloo, this was mid July 2016. We sat down and as the commissioner came in he looked me in the eye and said *"We want the Mckenzies".*

Music to my ears, I just wanted to know when we could get the deal out the way so I could get this show together. He spoke about the fresh season and what it was all about and said that the budget was not a lot for this pilot. I, of course, was used to this because I had pulled off a great show on small budgets many times. We established in this meeting that it was going to be a, 'Bentavision in association with Sugar films production'. Sugar belonged to Pat. The one term that I had to meet was to work with an experienced script editor. I hadn't done this before up until this point, everything I wrote was off my own back and I had never had notes before.

This was the start of another learning curve for me, but also with Pat's team at Sugar. This was their first scripted comedy, and it was my first-time experience going through a proper commission process for TV. I had my contracts looked over by my lawyer. This alone was a learning experience, I understood more about contractual terms and agreements.

The script editor that I worked with was a lady called Katie Mavroleon, who was the co-producer for *David Brent life on the road.* Working with her was fun as I saw the value of what a script editor was all about. Originally, I had pre-conceived ideas about networks and scripts editors, because I always thought that they would want to water down your script and take out the bits they did not understand. Although this may be true for a lot of people, but in this instance, it wasn't. What I thought they would get rid of they didn't, Having worked with Katie, she really made me think about things that I never would have thought, and I loved how she understood my world as a writer, and was able to look into my world from another perspective to make what I wrote better. I am all for script editors now! *Reader, this was one learning curve I had to overcome because prior to this, it was only me writing and being in my own bubble. I was very defensive of my work before. This experience helped me break out of that shell.*

When it came to casting, I had an issue. This pilot I was doing for ITV, would be the very first episode of Mckenzies that people would discover, so I had to start from scratch and write a brand-new script, there was a problem though.

Some of the cast I worked with before, I knew I wouldn't be able to keep. Firstly, there was the original actress who played Angel, she was now 16yrs old and could not play a 10yr old anymore so I had to replace her. The actress who played Charlene was away in China on a musical tour for another job, so she had to be replaced. As you knew from series 3 I had issues with the actor who played the dad, so I had to find a replacement. Adrian was dead, so the character, Ian, had to be replaced with another actor, this was hard to do but it had to be done. Casting with done professionally with a casting director. I emailed the casting director who cast me in Power Rangers and asked if she would do my pilot and she agreed. This was going to be a fun, but a tiring process, as there were a lot of actors to go through. I won't talk about the casting process in depth because it was very straightforward and we found the right actors for the roles. The hardest character to cast was the new Angel.

I had worked with children before, but because this was TV, compliance and legalities was also something my mind needed to expand upon. Working with children, they would require a chaperone and tutoring if they were filming on school days. They would also need to be on set for a certain number of hours and no more than that. I was the showrunner on this show and led the whole production and creative side of it. I arranged the crew and the casting and the locations of where we would be filming. Sugar dealt with contracts, compliance, children's licences, and arranged a post-production suite with a company called *Clear Cut.* Because the budget was so small, roughly £55k, there needed to be smarter ways of operating, and I knew that I would have to take on more responsibility at no extra cost.

The goal was a commissioned series which was what me and Pat were aiming for. Here was a list of my roles; producer, writer, director, actor, first AD, locations, costume for title sequence, and van driver carrying all the equipment. I also sought out a dance crew called 'IMD Legion' for the title sequence, as I wanted there to be dancers involved to put the icing on the cake for the intro. All in all, it was packed and such a short time frame to get things done, I wasn't pressured though because I was used to this, Sugar, however wasn't. *I'll explain more about this later.*

The filming dates were 4 days to be in mid-September back to back. 3 for the episode and one for the title sequence, the deadline for deliverables to ITV was early October.

August was the month for all pre-production and it was the ONLY month to get everything sorted. I had Shamara on board again, but this time there was no Niaz as she wasn't available. Sarah the makeup artist was back. The last time I saw her was in NYC when she was at the screening. My mum took care of all the catering and supported me throughout the entire process.

Casting had challenges. The dad I gave the role to accepted the part, but was offered another part for another show as it was emmy nominated. I was really annoyed about that, because we had gone through callbacks and readings with other actors by this point. This then made me request self-tapes from other options for the dad.

I also forgot to mention that at that point, *I flew out to Atlanta because I turned 30 this very same month! I had to review self-tapes whilst I was in Atlanta.* Most of everything had been taken care of before I left, and I was only in Atlanta for a week to then be back in London and clear up the last-minute dad casting.

I want to talk about my intention to go to Atlanta. I wanted to visit the Tyler Perry studios. He was an inspiration to me because he kind of reminded me of me in a sense as he too had been working on one idea for a very long time. Plus, I loved his whole ethos about studio ownership and greenlighting your own projects. This was something that I was into.

I had a friend I knew who lived out there and I also had family there too, once again family I had never met! *The Benta's are everywhere hahaha!* One evening whilst out there my friend and I attended a meetup and Tyler Perry's casting director *Rhavynn Drummer* was there. I thought that this would be my opportunity to get into the studio. Little did I know it was of no access to the public, but I didn't care. I hadn't travelled all the way from London to be disappointed. I spoke with Rhavynn and we literally met up the next day just outside the studios. We were both the same age. I wanted to get more info about this crazy talented guy called Tyler Perry, where the world would go mad over this brand called, 'Madea'.

We talked for about an hour and I learned that this man shoots 3 sitcom episodes a day. I was shocked! That's what I'm talking about! This is how fast I expect production to move when I work, ultimate productivity! Tyler set the bar for me for my future plans with BentaVision. As I stood by his studios, this man had his own studio police cars! I finished with Rhavynn and looked at the studios and wanted to get inside.

Myself outside Tyler Perry Studios - Atlanta 2016

I wanted to meet this man but he wasn't there that day, and I wasn't going to be in Atlanta long. Thoughts were racing round my head - I *had* to get in that studio to see the system of how this man worked. What's the worst that could happen? Get arrested for trespassing? *I could easily get out of that one! I could say I was from London, had a dream and was inspired by this man, wanted to personally say thank you and hand him these flowers (even though I didn't have any).* I made a decision... I was going to climb over the wall and break in! Sorry Tyler, my journey had been so friggin' stressful and I travelled from London to be here. Even if I got arrested it was worth it! I looked around and made sure no one was looking, I even looked at camera blind spots. That was it, I was jumping over. That's all I shall share about this experience in Atlanta, let's get back to London with the McKenzies.

I had about 4 more dads to look at for casting, which I had shortlisted whilst out in Atlanta. By this point, crew and other cast were already sorted and the dancers knew what they had to do. I was so grateful for this opportunity of working with Sugar, but little did I know that I would have to make a lot of corrections for certain things. I found myself having to double check what was done just so during production I didn't have any loose ends. It was really frustrating at times. I was moving so fast that they couldn't keep up with my pace. *I didn't understand it,* these were people who should be used to this more than me as they've collectively had more years in TV, but I took into account this was their first scripted comedy.

On a personal note, I noticed that the older generation of TV did not know *how* to work with a younger generation, who were more savvy and faster. They were adamant that their way was the way, which is understandable if you don't know anything else. It proved to me how the current TV industry operates, so much money was being used in areas where it wasn't necessarily needed, plus depending on who the talent was and who was running the show, the whole thing can move a lot quicker and money could be saved. I learned this from being at the Tyler Perry Studios! There were no excuses.

My roles were many, which can be *perceived* to an older generation as either *impossible, intimidating* or *too much* to take on. *Let me get this clear reader, nothing is too much to take on, it all depends on the 'mental capacity' of the person who leads the production.* Ignorance is advertised by the questions that people can ask. It's also advertised by saying you don't know another way of doing things. From working with them, I sensed they thought I was a bit naïve. I also thought that they would know a lot more of how to do certain things in production, but I found myself having to teach them, this young man had done work underground and had not only paid his dues, he was learning a new way, because that's what he was forced to do because he had to deal with a lot of 'NO'S from an industry. They weren't used to this fast way of working, and they were forced to learn from me.

All About The McKenzies, ITV2 Promo shot

I discovered there was a new way of working - a faster, smarter and more effective one. I had trained myself to be this way. I call it a generation of new breeds for the industry, a new generation of *showrunners.* I had literally trained myself all these years to be a showrunner and I didn't even know that's what had happened.

Filming was smooth with a bit of pressure so it kept me on my toes as I was manning all the days. There was one day that the commissioner and Sugar came down and they saw the process in action. They were impressed with how everything was put together. *Yes! That's what happens when you grind underground for years - you prepare yourself for the opportunity and you are underestimated!* I don't want to give off a negative impression about Sugar. That's not my intention. I thoroughly enjoyed the process and we both learned off each other! It was older and younger generation, TV and online coming together. I think a mutual way of summing up the experience was that we had teething issues, as it was a first for both of us in many respects. I value and appreciate them because if it wasn't for Pat's original meeting I would not have had the opportunity to do this. So, thank you, guys!

The ambience on set was warm and electric. Someone said that it felt like there was an invisible, unconditional hug. All the supporting artists really enjoyed working on the show and didn't want it to end, which is not the average response from an SA, considering they are on set waiting around for a very long time until they are needed. I just LOVE what I do! I want everyone that takes part in my productions to leave with a positive, loving experience, and feel that more life has been added to them.

It's important that we all love what we do. It makes you feel fulfilled and worthy and there's joy in it; there's a sense of purpose. You get out of life what you put into it, and I put my all into this show over the years and I finally felt things was moving in the right direction.

When it came to promotion of the show nearer the airdate, I had tweeted, Facebooked, Insta'd, anything I could think of to push the awareness of the episode. I asked the cast to do the same. What I noticed though was that I felt like I was doing most of it by myself. I wanted more help from Sugar, but sorry to say this, they weren't savvy with it. Don't get me wrong, the guys were great and I understood this was their first comedy, but I wasn't going to allow that inexperience to jeopardise my show. I had asked many people to retweet, and 1 out of 100 retweeted.

The show went live on ITV2 November 1st 2016 at 8.30pm. I sat watching it with my family. This was again history in the making as it was a black British family show being on screen for the British public. I felt proud and knew in my gut that this was going to be greenlit for a series, especially after the feedback I got from one of the commissioners when they saw the rough cut!

The show finished and I received so many messages from people, they enjoyed the show! I felt like a gap had been filled because this type of show is what people were longing for. I had WhatsApp voice notes from children of my friends, telling me that they liked the show and wanted more. Videos were recorded of little children dancing to the theme song and one was a 10yr old girl called Vanessa, who recorded a testimonial video giving her thoughts about the show - she was very excited and wanted more.

My heart was racing because this was what I wanted to serve a public that had been starved for years, to have my story told through art and ultimate creativity, to be a positive inspiration especially to the younger generation of the black community. We have had countless stories of gang violence, killings and young people getting locked up, I knew that my show would have a major positive influence.

So now that the show had gone out I was itching to know when ITV were going to ask for more episodes, I had no doubts in my mind - this was it for me. Everything I had wanted from 2011 when I originally did my pilot episode and it had been stolen.

In the meantime, Pat was reaching out to other networks for meetings, he said that striking whilst the iron was hot was the best way forward and not to leave all the eggs in one basket. Only one meeting came out from his efforts and that was with Comedy Central, from the offset I knew that Mckenzies wasn't right for them as they had already said that. However, they thought it wouldn't hurt for a meeting. Patrick and I went to their offices, sat down over tea and coffee, and heard what Comedy Central were looking for. Although it was good to meet them and hear what they wanted, I was more interested in what I wanted for a change. After all, *I put 6 years of my life into this shit and wanted a return from my efforts! But I sat there and listened.* It resulted in leaving our communication avenues open. I was all right for money for the time being seeing as I had received some payment from ITV. In my head, I knew they were going to ask for more episodes. I anticipated being able to get my own home, invest money into other ideas of what I wanted to bring to life.

Getting a series would catapult me financially. They sure were taking their time in getting back to us. It was the end of November and we hadn't heard anything back. It felt like London Live all over again, but I wasn't going to allow that to happen. I wasn't going to let myself be *'teased'* again, to be lifted and dropped back down, I had a lot riding on this.

Responses started to come back from other networks that myself and Pat reached out to, and they were rejections. I had to mentally hold ground and read what was said in emails. What I had seen were perspectives of mid-senior/ senior salaried, white men. Of course, I wouldn't expect them to understand a show like mine. *Was I affected by this? Yes, I was because considering there was all this hype about 'diversity', no one thought to take on a show that had already been screened to the public that ticked a diversity box and the people genuinely loved?! How was this to be explained?* I had attended another broadcast commissioning forum and all they spoke about was this topic and I sat in that audience and thought that these people were so blind! There was an answer that was evident and had been on their screens, why was this topic still being discussed about what to do about Diversity?!

What I took from these meetings was that commissioners and the decision makers didn't really know what they wanted. How can you hold meetings and say what you are looking for if you don't 100% know? I was up to challenge people though, especially when they said they were 'open' to new ideas and working with 'new' talent. Remember what I did with the BBC1 controller at the last event? I did it again but this time with the ITV drama department!

I managed to get a meeting with head of drama in ITV, following up a discussion we had at the forum. I thought why not speak to her and see if I can get some answers. Polly was her name, and I went back to the ITV building and had a discussion.

She didn't deal with the comedy department and the person I needed to see was on holiday! *Seriously, I'm waiting on an answer from that person and they were on holiday and never thought to tell me!? What kind of a system was this?!* As I sat in the office and looked around at all the show's pictures on the wall, all I saw was white people. From what was gathered at this meeting was what this woman wanted, and I got the impression that she wanted to do shows that *'she'* wanted to see and felt *'comfortable'* with. I remember one time reading in a book with writers, and there was a writer talking about networks in general. They said: *"We all respond to work that feels familiar to us, comfortable. Whether we know it or not. There's a shared aesthetic, a shared interest or sense of humour. As long as white men/women are making the decisions, then the majority of people they hire are going to be people who feel familiar to them".*

Just before Christmas of 2016, Pat called a meeting at his office. The news was that ITV were NOT going to be doing a series of the show. I died at this moment. It was like a sledgehammer hitting me in the face. I wanted answers as to *why*, because the woman who looked at the rough cut said that the show was perfect for the network!

Pat said it could have been several reasons but I wanted to know *'specifically'* why. He didn't have an answer and what hurt was the fact that he settled for that response! *There were no questions asked, no investigation! I guess it was easy for him to brush McKenzies aside because he never put 6 years of his life into this, he never sacrificed, he never went and lived in LA, he never went NYC, he didn't go through the blood, sweat, and tears that I had gone through this whole journey which was why it was easy for him to settle!* F*** THAT! I don't apologise for my language reader, this was serious shit! He may have wanted to settle but I wasn't! For a 6-year f****** journey I demanded an answer! I emailed the commissioner, I waited a week and no response. I emailed again, waited a week and no response. In January

2017, the commissioner finally responded to my email. This is what it said:

Hi Samuell,

I'm so sorry it's taken me this long to come back to you - I was out of the country over Christmas and came back to a mountain of work that needed immediate attention. Poor excuse I know but I hope you can forgive me.

I understand your frustration and I'll answer your question as best I can: I can't speak for Amanda but first, ITV2 changed its controller between the show being commission and its transmission. It was a decision that was made quite quickly due to unforeseen circumstances. The new controller had to make some quick decisions about the number and type of programmes he wanted on the channel going forward and he decided he didn't want to continue with Mckenzies as a long-term commission. Confidentially, he decided not to go ahead with any of the other shows in that season either.

Also, I watched the show as a 'punter' (I was still off work when the shows went out) and whilst I was really impressed with the high quality of the execution of the show, I thought it skewed a bit young for the ITV2 audience. In fact, I thought it would make a great kids' show but unfortunately, ITV2 or CITV are not currently in the market for kids' programming.

For both the above reasons, I'm afraid we'd not going to go any further with the Mckenzies.

I don't know if you're working with Pat and his team at Sugar on any other ideas but if you've got any other ideas you think might be right for ITV, I'd be keen to hear them.

Sorry not to have better news.

Best regards,

This didn't add up, because the other commissioner *'Amanda'* said the show was perfect for their channel! Fair enough they had another controller *(which reminded me of CBBC when I approached them in 2012 with Mary for the Angel Mckenzie idea),* but something still wasn't right here. What I was looking into was the commissioning and decision making 'process', I wanted to know how that system worked.

From going to a lot of broadcast commissioning forums and listening to commissioners, they speak very highly of *'discovering'* talent and being there from an idea's conception. Mckenzies was a different ball game. It was not in a position where a commissioner was there at its conception, because I travelled the unconventional route and did this myself in the underground. There's a lot of egos when it comes to commissioning, people in those positions want to be the person who discovered so and so whose show did amazingly well, they want to start off those people and launch those people, but with McKenzies. It was different, you didn't *start* anything, you didn't *do* anything, it was already made, developed and ready to go, so really there was no essence about it to stroke your ego, because you are in the back seat of the show's vehicle, not the front. It's a different perspective.

Remember people in those positions have a job and want to keep that job, they have bills, and they have salaries that they want to hold on to. Most people don't want to take risks as they fear they will lose their jobs, so they stick to *'what works'* in their eyes, but when you do that you block off new ideas and creative innovation, and new talent. Actors reading this, this is the same when it comes to casting, it's the path of least resistance, which is why you see the same actors over and over again. There's risk involved doing anything *new* or working with anyone *new*, and no one wants to be the *'fall guy'*, because they fear their careers will be over if they take a risk and it doesn't work. Job security. How long do we have to put up with these *'patterns'* of thinking in this industry? I sought to want to know more about this department.

I saw an opportunity with the creative diversity network. They had a commissioning development programme, which was a 12-18-month scheme to train talent in those departments. They were strongly requesting applicants from people of BAME, so I applied for BBC and Sky. I managed to get a reference from Pat which I thought would hold strong for my application. BBC rejected me, but I had an interview with Sky for the development executive role with the comedy department. The salary was handsome, and would have shifted things dramatically in my life where I could have finally left my parent's home from sleeping on the floor. I had done my research and made sure that I was on point for the interview which was going to be held with the head of comedy. On top of the application, I had two references and my own personal statement which I have copied for you to see below:

COVER LETTER: SAMUELL BENTA

01/01/17

To whom it may concern,

As a young man growing up I've always been interested in comedy. I love to laugh and grew up on many 90's sitcoms such as Fresh prince, My Wife and Kids, Desmonds, Only Fools and Horses and many more. I was always annoyed that on British TV there were stereotypical roles of people of colour and underrepresented people in the BAME community.

Starting off as an actor, this struck me as odd considering that the portrayed image was not in fact reality. Out of my frustration and zeal for change for British TV, I sought to change this by creating a family comedy called 'All About The McKenzies'. It started off online and one of the early 'webseries' back in 2012. Broadcasters still weren't interested in my ideas and I sensed they weren't savvy to the new generation of online shows and their creators. I never went to film school, in fact I was a self-starter who chose to learn the way into the industry and be a disruption... the unconventional route. Six years later my pilot for All About The McKenzies was broadcast on ITV2 on November 1st 2016.

I have had to face the embarrassment of being told that my show was 'too black' for TV, had many rejections and doors shut in my face, hearing comments like this made me hate my skin colour and I felt worthless at the time, but never stopped me. I posed the question to myself many times "what does it take to create huge success and have longevity in this industry?", "how can people of colour get their voices heard and be a great change maker?" I went out my way to research and analyse successful people. The word 'perseverance' kept on popping up and so I never gave up on my idea with my family comedy.

As I had no money my friend funded me so I had something to present to people in the seats of commissioning roles. There is one thing that I have learnt and that is this; many commissioners like to play 'safe', it's almost as if something must be *seen* for it to be *believed*. I strongly think that the new generation of commissioners should start taking risks on believing great ideas that can change the world, offering diversity and chances for new stories of comedy to be heard by the public. After living in LA last year due to wanting to get to grips of comedy and industry practice, I have grown to understand the difference in both language and cultural mindset in programming for TV. Being back in the UK with everything I have learned has given me insight into the gaps that exist here and the new range of possibilities.

I understand that I'm not at a normal level of your average applicant, however I'm the type of person who hasn't gone down the conventional route, I've paved my own way and learnt as I have gone along, seen things the conventional route would never have seen and met well established people who respected the 'earth is not flat' approach. Here's a brief excerpt from the BFI strategy: *"To support risk taking to influence this artistic evolution has never been so exciting. This broadening of cultural focus will be visible in all we do, as we set out in the next five years to inspire excellence, to ignite creativity, and to expand and deepen enjoyment of the moving image for all of us... A recent BFI taskforce found significant obstacles for those who choose to pursue a career in the film industry, and diversity in the workforce is poor. So, we are missing out on the talent and creative potential of a great number of young people that we really need for the future."*

I am young and pose the question of why not train up a younger person who brings fresh eyes, energy and insight? I have spoken on many panels in London, Birmingham and Manchester and LA regarding diversity and the invisible comedic stories that are out there but don't get a platform on mainstream TV. I am a keen learner and would love to work for such an amazing well respected company who can offer me the training to better my skills, engage me in and result in and result in commissioning brilliant comedy for TV and create history.

Your sincerely
Samuell Benta

That was what I wrote, I had to try and squeeze 6 years into one Microsoft word document when I applied. During the interview, the head of comedy and I got on very well. He had seen my show on ITV and said there was a lot of potential with it, but it wouldn't work for SKY. That's not why I was there. I was there to get this training opportunity. He wanted to know a bit about my journey so I told him.

His main concern was why would I want to be in a commissioning department after clearly demonstrating my passion for content creation. I responded that it would help give me a better picture of the machine, and there was a young fresh insight that I could bring to SKY and help them bring a younger audience to their network. I even had ideas about their scheduling and how to better engage this audience. He was fascinated and really listening to what I had to say, I even went to the extent of grabbing his pen and drawing a graph of where the industry was going. Who better to help you with engaging an audience online to your network than me. I'd practically grown on YouTube, it was a part of my DNA. He was blown away and at that moment I was confident that this training opportunity was mine.

I left feeling very confident and did my best not to give this opportunity much thought after the interview. My money was tight so I found a delivery driver job which was flexible, so it could allow me time to get on with other work. In the meantime, whilst waiting for a response I had been gathering plans together and researching successful American shows.

I wanted to start a writersoom, all American shows had them and I thought it would be an interesting avenue to explore and work with other writers. I wanted to take BentaVision to an extreme level of producing high quality comedies and dramas. I've always been fascinated with the big studios as they hold the ultimate power in the industry, so I was starting to look into Warner Bros and their history and see how they developed over the years to be one of the biggest companies for film and TV in the industry. Netflix and Amazon are household names for the online/app world for entertainment, so it was worth me looking into those companies as well. I invested into a lot of books and started to read up on these giants.

A month went by since the SKY interview and I was beginning to think what was going on, just like I had a gut feeling for ITV that I'd get the series, I had the same for this training opportunity. Surely after that interview and what I gave, surely, I'd get a call sometime soon. The scheme didn't start till March 2017 and it was already February at that stage. One morning whilst going over my plans for BentaVision, my phone rang with an unknown number.

It was the recruitment guy from SKY! My heart started racing and I was awaiting certain words to come from his mouth, but they weren't the words I expected. I didn't get the opportunity.

I sank to the floor whilst listening to the feedback, the head of comedy thought that I would better suit content creation than being in a commissioning department. I was angry because not only was I rejected once again, this was a TRAINING opportunity, and I had explained myself to the head of comedy of why the training would have been beneficial - it would have helped me gain a better understanding of the whole process and helped me in the future with putting together show packages. I also would have been an asset to them, as I brought a young unique perspective which would have been a gem in their team considering they had no one of my calibre currently!

Once the phone call ended, I literally stood up and said "F*** THE SYSTEM!, I'M GOING TO CREATE MY OWN SYSTEM!" For so long I had been trying to fit myself into someone else's system, and clearly from different channels they did not want what I had! I had put years of my life into this and I was so fed up of being shut out, even after PROVING myself, my talent, my skill, my impossible made possible evidence. WHAT THE F*** DID THESE PEOPLE WANT?! BLOOD?! This was a training not a job! I didn't understand it! ITV now SKY? *Really universe?! Are you going to do this to me again?!* This whole journey was an up and down stock market and I was tired of the f****** downs!

I had grown, I got better, I got faster, I got smarter and still it didn't stick out with these people.

I said I'm going to create my own system, a system where BentaVision is the network, we would be online and we would make the shows that broadcasters refuse to show, our quality will be so high that they would want to acquire the content that we have, we would house our own content just like what Netflix do, but we would be different, we would be better. We would also train a new generation of showrunners and build upon talent, develop them, nurture them, all of which a network does not do! We would also develop a new system for actors as well, the plans are coming together for a brighter future for ALL.

To check out the ITV2 Pilot of All About The McKenzies, type in YouTube: All About The Mckenzies ITV2 Pilot, or if you are reading an ebook click here.

I want to leave this chapter with a few lines I heard Tyler Perry say in a video I saw, he said *"Sometimes you are meant to be hidden, sometimes God will hide you, never despise small beginnings, there are things that can happen out of the smallest little start that can change the world, the great thing about being hidden is that you can be underestimated, you're able to do some things that not only change your path but the lives of millions of people. It will uplift and change everybody and everything. If you are struggling and fighting to be seen, sometimes you're supposed to be hidden, it's not your time to be seen yet, stay the course, learn what you can, walk in the path that you are supposed to at this time, and at the right time, God will reveal you, your talents and everything you've done to the world... in the meantime prepare..."*

PART 2

CHAPTER 8

THE BRIDGE TO PERSONAL DEVELOPMENT

So, there you have it, did you see the secret in the first section of the book? If not, that's ok, repetition is key. You witnessed an unexpected journey from a simple decision that was made in 2010. A decision where I wanted to create my own show, leading up to creating my own system for more shows with multiple showrunners, directors, writers and opening more acting opportunities for people like yourself. There was an evolutionary process, a process of manifestation *(which you will know more about in the next section of this book).* I started off just like most of you, an actor with one side of the diamond. You are an asset, you are a business, you are a commodity, but you need to build yourself to become more to have more and that takes a lot of personal development and understanding of who you are. There will need to be a lot of unlearning and relearning, dissolving old habits, and building new habits.

How many music artists do you know that are now acting? Did they start off acting? No, music was one side of their diamond that revealed another side to them as they progressed on that path, do you see a pattern? Look at British music artists like *Bashy (Ashley Thomas)*, who started off on the grime scene then moved into acting in films, and now starring in one of the biggest TV shows *'24 Legacy'*. *Stormzy* started off with music and he is now acting in films like *'Brotherhood'*. These are just a couple of examples but I'm sure you can think of many, I only spoke about those guys because they are British and have made a significant impact in the country. Writing this book for you is another side of my diamond, as well as the other sides I mentioned in this book. All grew over time once a decision was made to take charge of my life and create the life that I want.

The old days for actors was audition and wait for a phone to ring to see if you got the part. That's the only perspective that actors and agents can *see* because they don't know what happens beyond that point. I have shown you the other perspectives of what is shaping decisions in the 21st century. TV networks and executives are all about business, they follow the trends of technology and utilise followings of actors before they make their decisions. You want to build a following, a fan base, an audience you can guarantee is going to want to tune in to you! But to do that you need to start somewhere and discover more about who you are.

We are bombarded by too many distractions. Focus is what is needed and that focus will drown out the noise and distractions. I'm sure you have all heard the saying *'you get out of life, what you put into it'*.

What are you putting into it, other than waiting on a phone to ring? I can assure you 99% of the actors out there are waiting for that one phone call to get them their big break! This is 20th century thinking. You create your own break by taking charge and driving down the road less travelled. There's a reason it's *'less travelled'*, only the 1% go down this road and they succeed beyond heights the 99% can only dream for. As you saw from my story, it wasn't easy, but I kept on driving.

You may not even be thinking of creating your own show. I never said you had to, I only told you what I did. You could be a writer, an author, sing, rap, anything. As an actor if that's what you want to do, I would strongly suggest you cast yourself in a lead role in a show which highlights you. It is shocking to me to this day how many actors do not have decent showreels. You may say you haven't had any work to create a reel, but this is once again, 20th century thinking. CREATE SCENES AND GET THEM FILMED! You could get someone else to write a script or you can learn to write your own. You can find someone who has a camera or use your phone, the quality is good enough!

There are services for actors out there which deal with showreel creation and they will write and shoot scenes for you. Casting just want to see that you can ACT! If it's theatre that you enjoy the most, then write a one man/woman show and put it on at a theatre, invite an audience.

Do something different! If you do what you always do, you will always get the same results. You can't plant an apple seed and hope to expect bananas, you will be very disappointed all the time.

I want to get very real with you here, because I respect your life force. You are precious material, and there is NO ONE like you! You are one of a kind and no one can tell your unique story. You came here to play and show the world your talents and abilities. Time is ticking, haven't you noticed how fast the days are going?

Every year it seems to get faster doesn't it? Will you fail along the way, yes you will. You saw I failed many times! Did it stop me, no, why? Because my need to LIVE was bigger than paying bills! Don't let money or jobs stop you from LIVING YOUR LIFE AND DOING WHAT YOU WANT!

As I looked back on my life, I realised that every time I thought I was being rejected from something good, I was being re-directed to something better. So, what's the next step for you? If you want to create your own show I can show you how in another one of my books entitled, *'The Accidental TV Showrunner'.*

Part 2 of this book may be a bit heavy for some of you to take in at first, but I would be doing you a great disservice if I never shared with you this next important piece of information. The only thing that will make you resistant or switch off from the material, is what you currently believe about life and reality and what's true. Mindset is everything, the understanding and application of knowledge is the thing that gets results. Most people want results but they refuse to change their thinking, which is why they always lose. Thank you for reading Part 1 of this book.

Take a breather because you are about to dive deep and push the boundaries of your thinking.

CHAPTER 9

TO BE OR NOT TO BE

To be or not to be! We would automatically think of Shakespeare as an actor, right? But who really knows the depth of what was meant by these famous lines? To be successful or not be successful, we are human BEings, we are to 'BE'. Follow me carefully as I break this down for you scientifically. I care for you enough that I want you to realize what's going on in your head and your body. As actors, you should be used to this right? Maybe, but not the depth that I'm about to take you. I did say that I was going to share information with you that the average actor doesn't know. This is what's going to separate you from everybody else. The more you know *yourself* at a deeper level and understand how your mind works, it will make you a better performer and understand people more. Why do I mention this, and why is it relevant? Reader, do you drive? How often are you considering what's going on underneath the bonnet, hardly ever right? But don't you need the machinery under the bonnet to be in fully working order for the car to drive?

Have you ever said to yourself that you want to be successful? Or you want to become someone big no matter what you do? I'm sure lots of these statements have come out of your mouths at some point of time in your life. I have written this for you so you can understand a bit more about yourself and how powerful you truly are. We tend to look around and see other people shine and think to ourselves we can never be that big, *I can't do that, I can't afford it*, or my personal favourite it's *who* you know. Let me start off by saying that the most important person you need to know is YOURSELF, because once you know this then you will take more responsibility in your life. Knowing yourself is an ongoing process of enfoldment of what is already within you to be the greatest version you can be.

This next section of this book will dramatically change your life if you desire to study it further. This is information that you won't be taught in school and most likely will not be taught by your parents as they may not have been taught themselves. I have tried my best to write this as simplistic and straight to the point as possible for everybody to comprehend. Do yourself a favour whenever you come across a word you do not understand, please look it up in a dictionary and make sure you understand its meaning before you read on otherwise nothing else will make sense to you.

Take a look at your hands right now; really take a look at them. Analyse it look at them closely. Can you see the detail? Can you see the lines? Can you see the veins? Have you ever questioned why you are designed the way you are? Have you ever given thought to why you have 5 fingers and not 4? We take our bodies for granted and just accept them as *'normal'*, which is true, however you are a magnificent being above all creation. You are above all animals because you can create things with your wonderful mind. Take a look at the sky right now. Have you ever wondered why night comes after day or why there is a moon and stars? What is their purpose? Why do we have four seasons? Some people do not give these things any thought.

Think about it, for generations, people are born and people die but very few people are remembered. I'm sure you have heard of men such as William Shakespeare, Albert Einstein, Vincent Van Gogh, Isaac Newton, and the list goes on and on. These men have been gone for years but will always remain alive today in educational establishments because they brought to the world something great that left an impression on all of us. Did you know that you have the potential to be just as big as these historical giants? The question I should ask is do you *believe* you can be someone just as big? Whoever you are who's reading this, you may be tall, short, fat, skinny, black, white, Asian or whatever, you can have it all and live the life you want! Why? Because YOU said so!

I want to talk about YOU. Who are YOU and why are YOU here?

What I've noticed about people is most of them lack a definiteness of purpose, and they wander around aimlessly. If you look at every job role there are thousands! You have gymnasts, painters, carpenters, actors, singers, dancers, athletes etc. Look at what your amazing body can do. We are all unique and have something to offer this world.

I'm sure you have many talents that you are bursting to show everybody, but there are many of you who are very talented but do not have the confidence to push forward so you choose to conform to be classed as 'normal' to suit society and give yourself and others excuses for why you can't do it.

Many of you don't know *how* to achieve what it is you desire so you make no attempt at trying. We live in a world of television, radio, and Internet. Once upon a time we never used to have such a thing. Everything around you is a thing. Look around you right now and tell me something that someone did not think of. Look at what you are wearing, the device you are reading this book from, and the shoes you have on. Someone thought of it and made it. You never really gave that much thought, did you? You just went out and bought it because it either looked good or because everyone has it. Are you a bit more aware now?

Time and time again, I ask people *"can you tell me something that was never thought of?"* And they remain silent or there are a few that say to me, the *trees* or *water*. I totally understand their response, but believe me when I say trees and water are a creation just as you are. Everything has a part to play in this wonderful experience called life. Before reading the remainder of this book I want you to put the word impossible aside, remove all scepticism and be open minded as I explain to you why you *can* have what it is you desire regardless of what everybody says to you. My intention is for you to become enlightened and be more confident to go out there and do what it is you love and make better choices. You have a choice to believe or not believe what it is I'm about to present to you. As I recall there was a man who did say *"To be or not to be..."*

Although I was on my journey with acting from around 17yrs old, by the time I got to 21, I started to become curious as to why things were the way they were in life. I knew there was something about me that was special and that I deserved the best. *Have you ever felt like that, reader? Remember those times when you were younger and you knew exactly what you wanted to do?* I was fed up and was on the pursuit of self-discovery. My search began in books; I wanted to research the greatest people that ever lived, the people who made a difference to the world whether it was an actor, writer, inventor, or any occupation. From reading up on these people I asked myself the question what made these people so different? How did they become so popular? Why did they become so popular? Why they are still studied up to today? I had a burning desire to be the best I could be so after endless books, CDs, DVDs, and seminars, I started to notice a change within myself. I felt myself becoming more confident the more I focused on studying these people. There were lots of times I would lock myself in a room and passionately read for hours because of the zeal and enjoyment I had.

What I discovered was that these historical figures tapped into something higher. They all believed in a higher existence than us humans. There are many names for it; Universe, divine power, higher energy, but the most commonly used name is GOD. Now before you switch off on me you need to hear me out. These were the greatest that ever lived and contributed to society massively. This book doesn't intend to make you believe in anything you don't want to. I am merely just explaining the similarities in the beliefs of these great people. Before I started my path of self-discovery, I was ignorant to the idea of anything other than us dominating this world, but as I allowed myself to be open minded and accept new information my whole outlook on life changed.

Never have I been so curious and left unsatisfied with what I know now at the age of 30. I have not stopped studying myself, and never thought the day would come when I would be so fascinated with nature and wanting to know why, why, why and asking questions to how things happen.

How does a person become successful? Is there a formula? Is there assistance from a higher source that helps us? The questions never ceased. The whole reason I have put together this book is to not only show why acting is not enough in this new age, but to help you understand *yourself* more than you think and encourage you that nothing is impossible.

I want to be real with you and provoke you to think and ask yourself if you are happy with your current results. I can help you if you want to be helped. I'm no expert at what I want to share, but what I do know is that it can transform your life. This information did not come to me by chance but by years of diligent seeking for understanding.

Why should you read part 2 of the book? Interesting question, but the choice is yours; this book is merely a compilation of what I have learnt and understood over the course of my years and has helped me to do everything you have just read. I know that what I'm about to present to you will NEVER be taught to you in school, and I know how important this information is if you ever want to have an increase in understanding about how you work. I offer this to you, as I believe you NEED to know about the inner workings of your mind, so you know your responsibilities to having abundance in every aspect of your life. The key word here is *'choice'*.

Let's take an average day, you open your eyes, remove the sleep from them, and rise. Are you feeling alive or groggy? Do you know what today is? It's another day of either opportunity or failure. You go to the bathroom, brush your teeth, and have a shower. Now it's time to fix breakfast and if you have kids you'll most probably sort them out and drop them to day-care. You are going to head to work, school, college, or university whichever is your chosen route. You spend roughly 8 hours in those establishments, and then it's time to go home, but you are stuck in rush hour traffic and it takes an hour to arrive to your house or pick up your kids from nursery. Ah! sigh of relief, home sweet home! Oh wait... you need to make dinner, you put the TV on for the kids, and go to the kitchen.

The second scenario; Home sweet home, let me go onto Facebook, or do my homework, or play computer games. Couple of hours pass and It's that time where it's a date with yourself and the couch because its soap time. Let's discover people's miserable lives and see who's sleeping with whom and who murdered the villain. Episode over let's watch a bit more TV and then either bath or not. Bedtime now and you're either looking forward to tomorrow or not

The next day, open your eyes remove the sleep from them, and rise up. Are you feeling alive or groggy? Do you know what today is? It's another day of either opportunity or failure. You go to the bathroom and brush your teeth, and have a shower. Now it's time to fix breakfast.

Does this sound like someone you know? Quite a lot, maybe you have just read your life. Ask yourself; is this really what you want? Is this really what you were born to do? Yes, we all need school I'm not going to lie, we all need to know our times tables and adding, subtracting etc. Not a lot of us know where we are going in the long run. If you are a university graduate who is reading this then you may be struggling to get that job which you studied so hard for. You might say it's so hard to get a job. Then what do you do, you probably find any job you can get and eventually your degree meant nothing to you.

Let's really think, readers; from when we were little kids we were told we had to go to school, get good grades and get a job, for some of you this worked, for most of you it didn't. Some of you may be working in a profession that you don't like but it pays the bills. Some of you might like what you are doing, its *"good pay"* you say so you get comfortable and stay where you are. BEING COMFORTABLE IS A DANGEROUS PLACE TO BE! Your days are most probably no different than any other day. Are you comfortable with that? Are you looking for a way out?

Do you *believe* there is a way out? Have you ever heard anybody say *"only you can make it happen?" "Only you can make yourself successful?"*

We hear it all the time and it's great that people can say that to us, I totally agree with the statements but hardly anybody explains or shows us *how* it happens, *how do we become successful?* I'm going to show you how and it all begins with you and what you are. Notice I never said who, I said *"what"*. You know everything there is to know, you just need to remember.

So much is going on in the outside world, the media etc. We are surrounded by a multitude of different beliefs, opinions, and suggestions that it is complete mind chatter. What do you believe? What's right to you? Look at your life right now, and if it's not the way you wanted it to be ask yourself, *"Are you right?"* We all have something great in us; there is dormant power in you waiting to be tapped into and activated. You are here to serve the world with your talents and live a happy abundant life.

When compiling bits of information for this book I was baffled as to where to start so I thought by using the tree of life as a symbol and metaphor to what is going on in our heads. I've used pictures to help you visualize what I'm saying. I'm sure I don't need to tell you that we think first before we do anything. Some of us are not even aware of this; we simply react out of instinct for everything.

Take a look at the picture below:

Here you have a tree. We all know that a lot of fruits grow on trees; if you look deep down underneath the soil we will find roots. In terms of creation, this is where it all started for the tree. It was a seed that was planted; it sprouted into roots and grew as a tree. So, is it fair to say that what's underneath the ground creates what's above the ground? Yes. If we look at trees now we wouldn't even give thought to what was underneath we would just look at it and say, *"That's a tree".* We wouldn't say *"oh, that's a tree and there are deep roots underneath which determines how the tree will stand".* Do you the reader understand me? We wouldn't say that because we can't see the roots, they are invisible to us.

Let's look at the picture again:

So, there you have it. What's invisible creates the visible. The roots are hidden underground and create the tree. The tree is what we see and is what produces the fruit. This is how nature is, right? We plant seeds and they grow to produce a trees, which in turn produces fruit. This can go for any kind of tree or plant, or even as babies when they are born. They were once inside the womb hidden, and then they are born on the outside where we can see them. Most people live a very superficial way of life only based on what they see ABOVE the ground or in FRONT of their eyes. I am going to show you how we, as humans, are similar to a tree.

We are no different to nature, we are part of it. There's a huge part of us that exists that we are unaware of but controls every action we do and word we say. Do you the reader understand everything I have just told you? If not don't worry, we will dig a little deeper.

I remember when I was in school all we learnt about the human body was how many bones we had, and we had snippets of information regarding our organs, a little information on our blood but that was just about it, we then had to move on to a different scientific subject. Very little time was spent on knowledge about ourselves. I wonder why? What we are not taught in schools is that we live in more than one realm at the same time.

Some of you might think, *"What on earth is this guy talking about? Realms! it sounds like a computer game".* Bear with me as I give you a better understanding.

Take a look at this diagram:

We live in four realms simultaneously.

1) PHYSICAL
2) EMOTIONAL
3) MENTAL
4) SPIRITUAL

PHYSICAL

What most people don't understand is that your material world is your PHYSICAL, your OUTER WORLD i.e. you open your eyes and see everything around you; this is what we are most familiar with. It is everything 'above the ground' do you remember the tree? It's visible. Everything you see is a 'result' of something or someone that made it. Have you ever heard someone say to you something along the lines of 'by the fruit of your actions you will be punished?' The key word is 'fruit' as it's a result of the tree. Can you the reader read behind the lines?

EMOTIONAL

Emotions are something we feel; we have all had a range of emotions throughout all of our experiences. I won't get into a talk about this much but I'll touch on it a little. Have you ever felt so angry you wanted to smash something or fight somebody? Something triggered *'inside'* of you and you felt the experience of an angry emotion all over your body. The key word here is *'inside'*. Yes, this emotion was inside of you, you felt it but it wasn't a physical thing like your hand. Emotions are intangible they are in you and not outside of you. You can express an emotion that will make you do something which coverts or crosses over to the physical. An example of this would be to be angry with somebody and physically hit them or feeling lust for somebody and physically having sex with them. It is very important that we learn to control our emotions; I'll talk more about this in a later chapter.

MENTAL

This is an area of study that we know little or nothing about. We take the word for granted, but do we actually know what it means? We understand that mental is something to do with the mind *'inside'* our heads and that's pretty much it, but your mind is in fact, *not* inside you head, how do you know? Have you ever seen the mind? Did you just think of your brain? Your mind is not your brain! You will discover that the mind at its deepest unconscious level is not in our heads at all. In fact, it's our whole body if you break it down to the cellular level. Unless you are a psychologist or scientist you will most probably remain ignorant to this word called 'mental'. I mean ignorant in terms of *'not knowing'*. I must tell you that the enormity of this realm is unlimited in terms of information. It is huge and I cannot explain in this book everything about it due to the amount of information, but I will explain as much as I can. I am not looking to overload you in a way that you will switch off. You can look at many videos on this subject and there is much you can find in books.

Whatever you do, do not think of the McDonalds logo!

What happened? You just thought of it, didn't you? A picture of the logo popped up in your head, or an experience or memory of McDonalds flashed before your eyes just as you read the word. You don't physically see McDonalds but you saw it mentally. Is it fair to say that you saw it in your 'INNER WORLD?' Do you the reader understand where I'm going with this? Let's go back to the tree. Remember we talked about the roots being under the ground and that the tree was above? Let's look at you. Your body is above the ground you can see it, but your emotions and mind is below the ground, it's inside of you where you can't see it but you feel it. Do you see the similarity with the tree and us? Now let's put this information in the diagram.

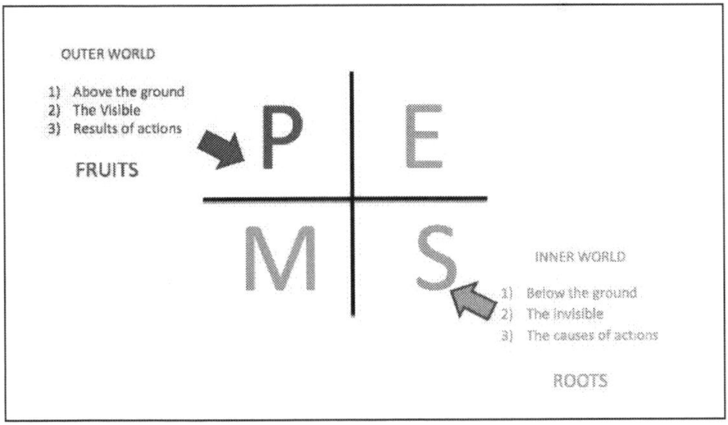

If you look carefully at the diagram, you will see that the inner world is a lot larger than the outer world. I have highlighted the inner world blue and the outer world as the colour red. Why is this inner world a lot larger? Notice that I have left the SPIRITUAL blank for now as it will be explained as I talk about this wonderful thing called the mind. We all have a mind and there are two parts to it, a masculine and a feminine side. There is a conscious mind (masculine) and a subconscious mind (feminine). We know that we have an inner world and that it's not a physical thing that can be touched. I'm sure you all have had a moment when you daydream or you think about something that happened previously, or something you imagine is going to happen. All this is done in your mind.

CHAPTER 10

THE SCIENCE OF THE ACTOR'S MIND

I thought it be best that I start off with the subconscious mind, which is also known as your emotional mind. From what I have discovered this thing we call the subconscious is what determines what happens to us in life whether it's good or bad. Let me explain. All actions we perform with our body stem from the mind. We think a thing first and then we do it. The question is why do we do it? What makes us do it, even if we don't want to? And more importantly how do we change it if we don't like it? This subconscious mind accepts any information you give it and will produce what you present to it.

The Hard-Drive

I want you to think of your computer. Let's say for example you type up an essay, save it and then switch off the computer. Now switch it back on, you can easily load up the essay and see what you had written before. The essay was saved on your hard-drive. Our subconscious mind is no different than the hard-drive of your computer. In fact, it is better than your computer. From the moment we were born, our minds have been constantly active recording information from the outside and stored in our subconscious.

There is no limit to how much information we hold. We are unlimited; we are not like hard-drives where you have 2GB, 8GB etc. It's like a huge library holding everything you've experienced in your life. The ironic thing is, most of us would not even attend a library unless we needed to find a certain book for studying, not knowing that we are a walking library of experiences.

We think in pictures as we have already discovered when I asked you not to think of the McDonalds' logo. It's impossible not to think of it because the word is attached to a picture, and depending on what the word or picture is, there could also be an emotion and experience attached to it as well.

I am going to make you visit your own human library. I do not know you, reader, but I am guessing you've had a bad experience with a certain someone in your life, maybe there are numerous people. Did that person/people just pop up in your head? How would you feel if I asked you to keep that image in your head for about two minutes? Depending on the severity of the experience you had with that person, an emotion would emerge and you would probably get angry or start to get upset and cry. Emotions are controlled by the thoughts you entertain.

Who was your first kiss with?

1) One of two things has just happened... either the person justpopped up in your head automatically OR you had to think for a moment, search through all the pictures of people you've kissed to locate the image of that very first person.
2) Now you are thinking of the actual experience you had, or if you're not, now you are. You remember where it happened, when it happened and probably what else happened that day prior to you doing the act.
3) Depending on the experience, you will either smile or not want to think about it as it was not so nice

What kind of music do you like? If you like rap/RnB, what artists pop up in your head? Can you hear a certain song playing in your head now? We can remember songs so easily, even if we have not heard them for years. We will remember the beat and the lyrics, and then we will probably start singing that song. We would probably even picture the music video in our heads.

Let me take you a bit further back. When we were babies, we were taught to identify pictures and attach words to them for e.g. cat, dog, spoon, bird, chair. Do you get the idea? Those of you that are mothers or fathers who are reading this can understand where I am coming from as you have probably taught your own kids. Do you understand what I mean by you are a walking library of experiences? We think in pictures!

If you are having difficulty studying a subject it is because you do not have a picture that corresponds to what is written in the text book. That is why certain subjects baffle you in school because you don't understand what the teacher is saying or not understanding what you are reading, because there is no picture to attach it to. If there is no picture, we experience what we call confusion. Anything anybody says to us, we automatically picture what they are saying because as they speak words, we are automatically attaching pictures to their dialogue. Believe me when I say, whenever you are confused, it's because you do not have an image or chain of images that link to the information being presented to you by someone. I will not go further into this but the whole point was to show you that you "remember", and that pictures and experiences are saved in that wonderful hard-drive called your subconscious, and don't worry, it can never be erased unlike these material computers that break or accidentally erase and you can never find the information and you need to start again. Did you just picture a time where your work got deleted? Nothing compares to your subconscious.

Beliefs/ Habits/ Paradigms

I'm going to move onto beliefs, but I shall get more into detail regarding this when I move to the chapter of law of attraction. I just want to note that when I say the word belief I am not talking about religion. I am talking about the word itself. People tend to hear the word belief and immediately think religion (remember what I said regarding pictures, words are attached to an image?). Belief is the psychological state in which you hold a proposition or premise to be true. Do you understand this? Let me explain it a bit more in detail.

If you are a female reading this and you've had bad relationships, you might believe that "all men are the same" or "men only want one thing". How many times have you said that or heard someone else say that? Probably quite a lot, this is an example of a belief. Let me give you some more examples: *"I can't afford it", "we don't have enough money", "I am so broke", "money doesn't grow on trees"*, etc.

A belief does not just represent money but it could be about anything. Beliefs are so powerful that any action or decision you make will be based around that belief or point of view. Your beliefs are the foundation of your thoughts just like a blueprint is the starting point for a builder to build a house. Your action is the building, your thoughts are the blueprint. Do you understand? All your thoughts stem from what you believe. The problem is, a lot of us are unaware of what our beliefs are. They are so deep down in our subconscious mind that we automatically act according to it. When we experience anything, it leaves an impression on our brain that in turn will be recorded in our subconscious as "experience". We will remember the sensation around that experience whether it's good or bad, which will determine whether or not we do it again. Let me ask you this... Why do you listen to a certain song over, and over again? It's because you like it, right? Why do you like it? Was it the lyrics? Was it the beat? To your knowledge, you would say *"yes"*. The more we repeat something over and over again, it will become a habit and the more we keep up the habit, the deeper the roots will grow deep in the subconscious. I'll speak more about this later when I show you another diagram.

Paradigms. This is the beast that will keep you where you are, the decisions you make and what makes you make excuses for not doing or doing certain things. A paradigm is a multitude of habits and ideas. A paradigm was created in you right at the point of conception when you were formed in the womb of your mother. Your parents' beliefs were genetically transferred to you to a certain extent. This is why you may speak and act like your mum or dad. This is why you may have a similar personality to your mum or dad. Your mum's way of thinking or your dad's way of thinking could subconsciously be your way of thinking, which you may be aware or unaware of. Paradigms control what you're thinking. You are a product of someone else's habitual way of thinking. School has you programmed to believe that if you can repeat something then you've got it. That isn't so because you can repeat stuff but the paradigm controls the behaviour. Yes, you may remember times-tables and 1+1=2 but I'm not talking about that.

School didn't teach you how to alter a paradigm to change behaviour; they would just punish you and expect you to change. I.e. you say you will stop smoking, you stop for a while, you're all right for two weeks then you go back to smoking. Is this familiar with some of you? You may have had a moment in your life where you so badly wanted to start doing something different. You start it for a short period of time and then you quit, for e.g. you may have wanted to take up karate lessons, you got started and then you switched off after about a couple of weeks. You then made up excuses to why you weren't doing it anymore. This is your paradigm! It is controlling you and keeping you to where it was comfortable for you.

I'll give you an example of myself: Ages ago I wanted to bulk up in the gym, I was so excited and told myself numerous times that I was going to keep it up. I was in the gym, I was eating and I noticed great improvements within weeks. Around the eighth week, the amount of work in the gym was starting to slack and I came up with excuses to why I wasn't doing much. I did fewer exercises, fewer weights and then I stopped going to the gym. I convinced myself that I would be all right doing press ups at home, so I did these every day, then it dropped to every two days and then eventually I stopped. My eating went back to how it was usually and now I'm back to square one. This was my paradigm! It held me where I was 'used to'. It wanted to keep me in my comfort zone. *Check out this video of me doing a presentation to an audience regarding comfort zones. In YouTube type in: Samuell Benta – The danger of a comfort zone. Or for ebook click* here.

Do not be fooled by this statement as it separates the winners from losers, the motivated from the demotivated. Strong will power is what is needed to work through these paradigms to get them to shift. The whole idea is to create new habits using repetition that will form a new paradigm and then you have reversed the situation. The key word here is *'repetition'*. Scientists have gone on to say that it takes 30 days to create a new habit. Our brains receive an impression from the first act, then repeated acts develops new neuronal connections and every time that act is repeated the connection and wiring of these connections get stronger, and thus creates a synaptic connection/habit.

Whatever you eat, drink, watch, touch is not necessarily a conscious decision, what you tend to gravitate to is what you are habitually used to. You have the ability to accept or reject certain information that enters your subconscious. I guess you can call it the bouncers at the door of the club, it decides who's going in. Remember me telling you the subconscious is the feminine aspect of the mind? Well, the conscious mind makes the decision of what enters the female. Take a look at this picture:

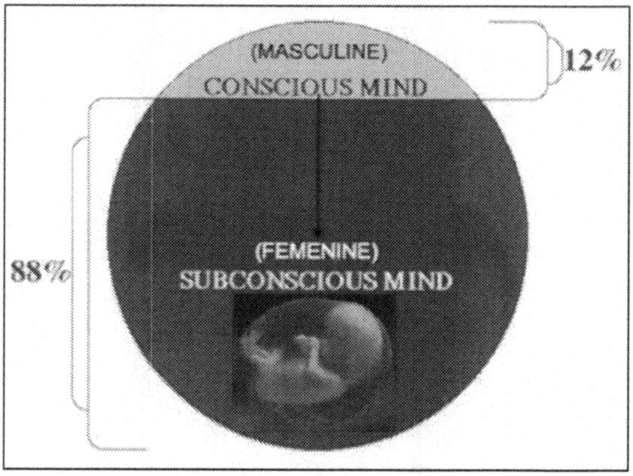

I'll bet you haven't seen this picture before? Let me explain. Notice that the conscious mind is smaller than the subconscious. If we think of a male impregnating a female, the female would produce the baby. Male and female must work together to produce a baby, women cannot get pregnant alone. If you look at the sex of some animals the female would always appear larger. These are animals that are physical, but I'm talking about the mind, it's the same principle but it's invisible, *more about this in the chapter Universal Laws – Law of Gender.*

Whatever you consciously project onto the subconscious, will produce a result. What exactly do we project onto the subconscious? It's thoughts and ideas! Thoughts originate in the conscious mind, which either gets rejected or accepted. If accepted it gets passed down to the subconscious which believes what you project onto it, why? Because the subconscious believes anything you project onto it. It doesn't know right from wrong and it doesn't judge. Only the conscious mind has the ability to judge. Let's get more in depth.

We've identified that we think in pictures and that words are attached to pictures. We are constantly thinking whether we know it or not. If you are having trouble in any area in your life, you are responsible for the results! Are you offended? It wasn't my intention, but I will be real with you, you are responsible for the results in your life whether they are good or bad. Ignorance is what the problem is, we do not know about ourselves which is why we get ourselves into so much trouble. I'm talking every aspect of your life whether its relationships, finances, or health. I am going to show you a scientific formula below which is immutable and cannot be broken which could probably change your life if you choose to study it further.

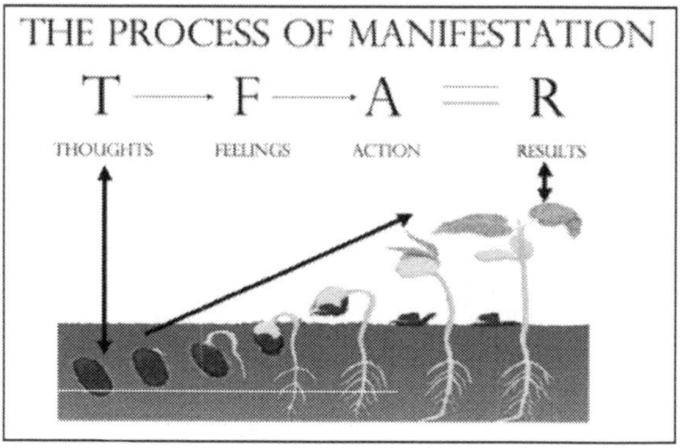

This is the process of manifestation. Everything begins with a thought. The thought dictates how we feel, and how we feel will control how we act. How we act will produce the result. In this picture, you can see a picture of a seed planted and it sprouts and grows through the soil producing a flower. Thoughts are seeds, we already know that thoughts are invisible hence the reason they are in the soil in the picture. They are in the ground where we cannot see them, but they operate exactly like a physical seed. Ask your science teacher and they will tell you that all seeds have a gestation and incubation period. There is a period of time before the realization of a planted seed. It's like our thoughts - there's a period of time before the physical realization of an idea. Everything we see around us started in thought, and is now a physical thing to be realized. It was created in the conscious mind first as an idea, then it was projected onto the subconscious which produced the result and then it was realized outside. Remember the tree? It started with the seed, the roots, the tree and then the fruit. It's a process. It's the same process with our thoughts.

A moment ago, I mentioned that we are responsible for the results of our life. Look at the process of manifestation at the results. We tend to always look at results and complain about them and we tend to blame people, events, and circumstances for the outcome. We are either living in ignorance or knowledge, to some extent we are living in both. There are things we know and there are things we don't know. If we do not know the process of manifestation, we're in trouble because it is this process that governs our lives. If you are having a bad relationship right now, it can get better if you use this process correctly. Let's say for e.g. love is dying in your relationship and you are losing interest in your girlfriend or boyfriend. Did you know that you are responsible for the outcome of that relationship? We tend to wait around and expect people to change to suit us. This is not right. It's in violation of many universal laws, which we shall discuss later. The result of your relationship right now, if you are not happy, you can change it by using the process of manifestation. We tend to fight the 'results', but there is a process. It starts with thought; we need to 'think' of a different approach to 'act' differently to get a different 'result'. Stop waiting on he or she to make the first move because you may be waiting a while. We tend to leave a relationship when we don't get what we want. That is lazy and selfish. Attitudes need to change and that attitude can only change when you know the correct information about yourself, and this will then give you the realization that you are literally responsible for changing your results.

Think about this for a moment. Who taught you how to kiss? Who taught you how to have sex? I doubt it were your parents! You learnt how to do this from getting the idea from an outside source, most probably from TV, movies, or friends. Why have I mentioned this? It's because it's a powerful example to use in terms of where do you get your ideas? Did you create the idea or did someone give it to you? Let's go back to beliefs, where did they really come from? Are they someone else's or your own? We could be subconsciously living the lives of someone else's ideals without realizing it. We need to ask the question why we believe what we believe. Where did the source of information come from? Where did it originate? The further back we study, the more to the truth we will uncover.

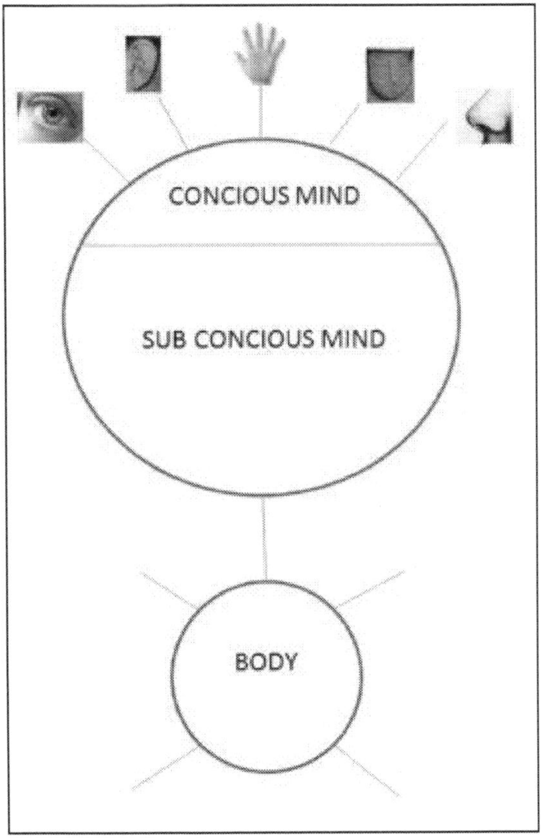

What does the mind look like? There is no image, as it's not a physical thing to see, but I will draw you a picture to help you best understand based on the information I have already given you. We think in pictures so we need a picture to operate with. This picture was originated by Dr Thurman Fleet back in 1938, who dealt with the healing arts.

If we imagine this picture, as a stick person with a very big head, the top half of the head is the conscious mind and the bottom half is the subconscious. The lines on top of the head are like little antennae that pick up information through the 5 senses: see, hear, touch, taste, and smell. That's how we are living now, everything we do are based on decisions that are senses dictate whether consciously or subconsciously, and this is where we can be misled if we do not have the right information, ideas, and concepts. Who is making your decisions? Who does your thinking for you? We are constantly receiving information and suggestions from people all around us. If you are watching the news on TV, you'll be hearing all sorts of dark, negative information and we can choose to either accept or reject that with our conscious mind.

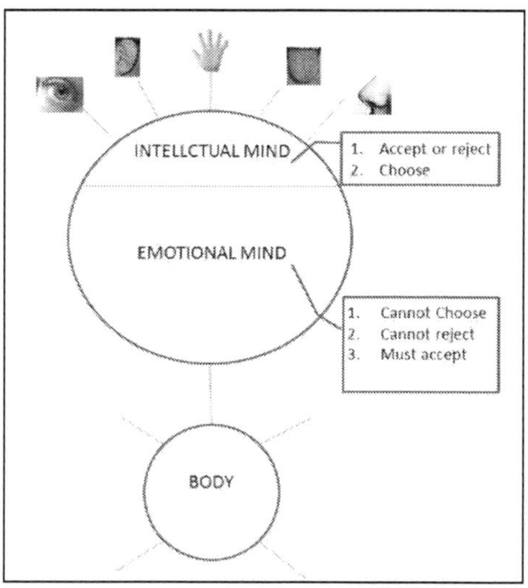

The problem a lot of people experience is accepting any and everything from all sources leaving you confused. What makes you think that what you see and hear is the truth? We are constantly getting into fights and arguments by choosing to believe what we receive and we don't even think to investigate or re-evaluate those ideas. The fact that we fight means we are not using our mental faculties effectively as are feelings make us do wrong to others, but we can control that thinking from the correct knowledge and understanding of ourselves. What we need to do is consciously work on improving and developing our higher mental faculties. What are they you might ask? There are six higher mental faculties and we all use them to a certain degree.

The six higher mental faculties are:

Perception

We constantly perceive what is going on around us. We are interpreting everything. Have you ever had an argument with someone and said something for the person to say *"that's not what I meant you've gotten it all wrong?"* This is an example of perception, you believe you are right from your point of view and the other person believes they are right from their point of view. There are always two sides to a story and neither is wrong or right, it's what works that's what counts. You may perceive an experience to be bad when in fact it is neither bad nor good depending on the meaning you give it. Can you, the reader, understand what I am saying? Nothing is good or bad but your thinking makes it so. Its polarity, there are two ends to the pole. I may dip my foot into a pool of water and perceive it as hot, but you may do the same and perceive it as cold. Who's to say who's wrong or right? It's a matter of perception. The more we study and understand ourselves and the way nature works, the larger our awareness will expand and what we perceive will be a lot more nearer to the truth. We will react less and respond better because we have a deeper understanding on this word called perception.

Will

The will is our ability to concentrate. It's the ability to hold one idea on the screen of our mind to the exclusion of all outside distractions. Have you studied with a lot of noise going on around you with people talking? You are using your will power here. If we are determined at anything you can be sure you are using your will. It's will power that allows us to keep on going regardless of obstacles that get in our way. Some examples of people who have had strong will power are Adolf Hitler and Napoleon Bonaparte. They may not have been the best role models but they had such a highly developed will that it influenced a mass majority of people. The power of the will helps you keep going regardless of setbacks, rejections, and hardships. This is something to be achieved, if you develop this faculty nothing can stop you from achieving your dreams.

Imagination

We have an excellent imagination. Everything begins first here. In order to make something we have to imagine it first. Children are excellent at using their imagination, but as we get older we tend to use it less creatively. If I said to you to imagine yourself sitting on a camel and riding through the Sahara Desert, you'd be able to do it as you read these words. In fact, when you read any way you are using your imagination, read a storybook and you'll see a movie playing behind your eyes. Most of what happens to you in life has been the result of your imagination. Have you ever had a time where you imagined something was going to go wrong and it did? What if I said to you that you had a part to play in that event going wrong, just by imagining it? That may be a tough concept to accept but as you study this further you will be more conscious of what you choose to imagine. *More to follow in the chapter of law of attraction.*

Memory

We have an excellent memory! We just haven't been taught how to develop it. We should be able to recall anything we want in seconds. That's not the case with a lot of people though. How many times have you heard someone say *"I can't remember"* or *"I've got such a bad memory?"* Probably quite a few. This isn't so, we have an excellent memory, which can be developed just as if we were going to go the gym and start pulling weights to develop muscle. Can you imagine a life where you can recall things as and when you need it? As an actor, don't you need to recall lines from memory?

Intuition

Intuition is our knowledge (Inner voice). It's what we understand to be true, or what we use to judge right from wrong. I'll give you a test. Study as much as you can about yourself and nature and your intuition will increase and understanding will deepen where you can read people like a book. Where others are complaining about their lives and their issues and not understanding why it keeps on happening. You understand secretly. If intuition is our knowledge, ask yourself, has your knowledge got you the results you wanted? Remember this, what you reading here are new ideas, which will benefit you if you keep studying, expand your knowledge, and understanding, which will expand and deepen your perception. A harsh truth for all of you but it has to be asked, did your current knowledge and hard work get you your results that you *'wanted?'* Did you get your dream job? Yes or no? If no, then I ask you to expand your intuition, which will give you more options and alternatives.

Reason

Reason is our thinking. It's what is also known as our rationality. You may think smacking someone is rational. This is true to you; you believe this is right. This is your reason. This is the faculty where thinking comes from one idea to a related idea. But more specifically, it is the way we consider explanations concerning what's true, false, good, or bad. This is where our paradigms come into play; remember what I said a paradigm was? It's a multitude of habits and ideas, so how you think influences how you will behave in any given circumstance. Perception also determines how we think, all faculties work together. They are intertwined and work together in synchronicity. Have you ever taken the time to consider *why* one thought leads to another, and who decided it was the correct sequence? We are all unique and process information differently. Either way we have the power to choose how we think.

All a bit too heavy for you? Or are you enjoying reading this? You will know the truth when you hear it. We already know everything there is to know, it's just we have forgotten. I have touched on the conscious, subconscious and our mental faculties; now that you know what they are you should do yourself and the world a favour by developing them to the best of your ability, so you can *become* more and add more value to your chosen field. I have to mention again that you are an amazing creation and you were made to create. You're creating your own lives as you go about your days. It is important for us to spend most of our time on what it is we want to produce. We think in pictures, and the mind works with pictures all the time. Be honest with yourself when I ask you this question, *"What do you constantly think about?"* You may not even know, because most of us aren't aware that we are thinking. We literally just go about our days doing actions as we see fit. We listen to music, watch TV, have a gossip, and hang with friends talking about all sorts, not paying attention to what we are planting in our mental soil. Remember the process of manifestation? I'll show you the picture again:

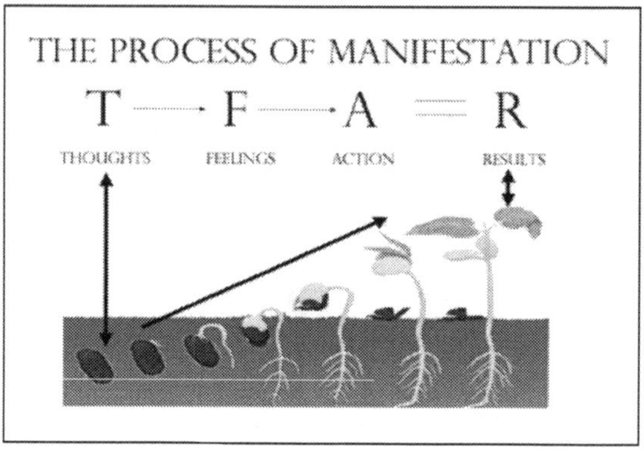

Thoughts are seeds. We are influenced by people to a certain degree depending on the strength of our mental faculties. If we do not learn about ourselves and the way the universe is governed, we are doing ourselves a huge disservice. If our intuition does not get fed the right knowledge we can easily be swayed by people's opinions and accept anything that comes to us, we will worry, get depressed and upset and live in fear. If you picture your mind like a house, you would know that a house needs to be stable, secure with a roof so rain doesn't get in, and strong enough so that the wind does not blow it down. With the right knowledge comes correct understanding, which leads to wisdom resulting in a more courageous, confident person. Is that the person you want to be?

I'll tell you right now that there is NOTHING TO FEAR IN THIS WORLD! Ignore what they say on the news, do not accept negative information. Move away from negative company. Seek for knowledge, wisdom and understanding. The fact that you are reading this right now is not by accident. This is the starting point of a great life for you as something inside of you awakens, or it may be encouragement for those of you who are already on this path.

It is mentioned by scientists that we only use a tiny percentage of our brains. We have infinite potential! There's no end to how good we can be at what we do. Look at what we have accomplished as humans. Take a look around you, everything was created by someone! Someone thought of it! YOU yes YOU can DO and BE what you want. It is promised to you, and I'll help you by introducing you to laws that govern our being and everything around us. You may have noticed about yourself whilst reading that there is a side of you that likes what you are reading, and on the other hand there may be a little resistance with certain points raised, this is understandable as right now your thoughts, values and beliefs are quite varied. You are in the process of rewiring your brain, as your thinking changes so does your decision making. If your thinking weren't already changing, you would not be reading this book. I want you to forget about your hardships, they do not serve your current thoughts.

Even in my 9th year of being on the path of self-discovery, I have always wanted to find out a specific process of eliminating past baggage mentally, so I can be as efficient as possible. I noticed with myself that I got hype reading personal development books, so took action, and then over a period of time I digressed and went back to the old self of behaviour. It left a pattern in my life that I hated and I needed a permanent change for consistent successful results in all areas of my life. I hate it when I see so many people who want a better quality of life, they have the best intentions, but it seems like they are pushing a huge boulder up a hill and then it keeps on rolling back down. That's because although they consciously want to move forward, they have subconscious beliefs that are so buried deep within the psyche and conditioning of the cells of their body that they keep backsliding - it's like having one part of you that wants to move forward and the other half saying no you are not.

You have thousands of decision-making strategies running through your mind every day, everything you do is based on a strategy. Wouldn't it be great to know what is going on inside yourself and how you can create harmony within both parts of your mind and have the habits, traits and qualities of an effective, successful person living an abundant life following their dreams? Take a look at the picture below to get an idea of how information passes through us:

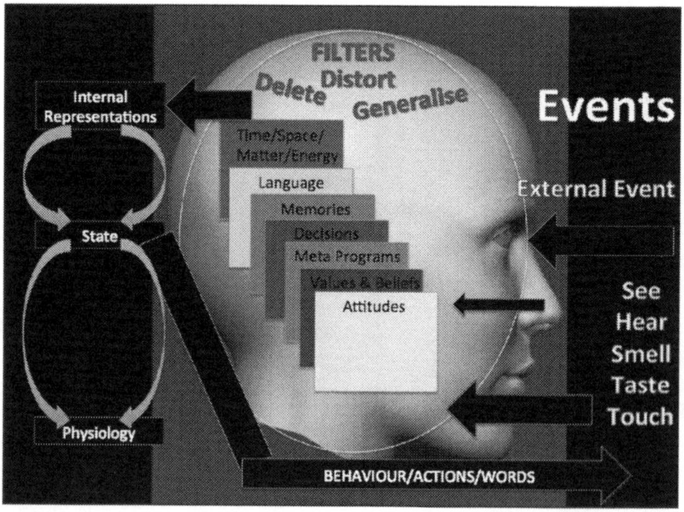

Isn't it shocking how much information we were not taught in school? I bet you think by reading this section of the book that you are in a science lesson, and it has nothing to do with why you picked it up in the first place. Just think how far advanced you would be now and how much trouble you could have prevented yourself just by knowing this information from a younger age. This is why I am so passionate about getting this information out there. I don't know who will resonate with me but what I do know is that this book will reach the right people at the right time in their lives. Some of you reading this may never have heard of me and that's ok because by the law of attraction you have attracted this book into your life as the next piece of your puzzle.

In the next chapter, we will be looking at Universal laws and their core importance in your life. I stumbled across these earlier on my journey and after I have explained them I show you an example of how these laws have helped me in my life so you can see how they actually work. The beauty about these laws is that you will notice how they work with your being.

CHAPTER 11

UNIVERSAL LAWS

This is the section of the book where you will either be fascinated or sceptical, the choice is yours. Remember what I said about the conscious mind? You can accept or reject or neglect what I'm about to say. I ask that you do none, and examine the ideas and new information and then choose for yourself. Only a fool would not examine an idea. Do you want to know why people are sceptical? It's because a new idea challenges what you currently think to be true. Ask yourself, is what you think to be true getting you the results you want? If not, please open your mind and investigate. What I present to you now is not my own made up concepts but can be proven by top scientists today.

"The natural laws of this universe are so precise that we don't have any difficulty building spaceships, we can send people to the moon and time the landing with the precision of a fraction of a second... these laws must have been set by someone... "– Werhner Von Braun

This universe moves in such a precise order and as we gain an understanding of that order, we can move our thoughts and actions into harmony with it and live a fulfilling life. What are universal laws? First let's define the word universal, there are many definitions of this word but I want to emphasize on the definition: *"Of, relating to, extending to, or affecting the entire world or all within the world".* From what you have read so far, this book I have I have talked about your 'inner world?' You are a spiritual being inside a physical body, but your body is inside of a huge universe. Everything is connected.

An example of a universal law that you have been taught at school is the law of gravity. You've heard of Sir Isaac Newton. We all know that if we run off a cliff, we will fall off. We know if I throw something up, it will come down. This is a law, but its invisible we cannot see it. The only visible law we can see is the police force or court system, but these are man-made laws. Universal laws are God laws. Laws, which cannot be broken and will either reward or punish you. These laws are what govern every person, situation, and circumstance. They are not new laws that have been invented. These are laws that have always been here since the beginning of time.

LAW OF VIBRATION & ATTRACTION

The law of attraction is as simple as like attracts like. Like energy attracts like energy. We think in pictures. The images you hold in your mind are what you attract. You are a walking magnet. Everything that's going on in your thinking is what you attract to you. I'm sure you walked into a room and felt a bad vibe off people; you didn't want to be around them, did you? You weren't attracted to them. Whatever you focus your attention on, you attract. A thought repeated consistently is what shows up in your life, whether it's good or bad.

If you are constantly thinking about bad things that have happened in the past, you will attract likewise now and in the future. Everything that comes to you in your life, the people you meet, and the events you go to, the situations you get yourself into, the weird circumstances you find yourself in - you attracted! This may seem a bit mystical to some of you who are reading but I'm not asking you to believe me, I'm only presenting information to you and if you choose to study it further I promise you will notice changes in your life.

We talked about the subconscious mind producing your results, but how? Did you ever ask that question? The mind is not physical, if a thought starts in the conscious and projects onto the subconscious this will determine the vibration we are in and dictate what we attract. The thoughts you think. travel and affect this whole universe to suit you. I'll give you an example. Have you ever thought about someone and then that person rang your phone, or you saw them in your travels? You created this! Yes, you did, it was no accident. Thoughts are things! Think back to what I said about beliefs, your actions and viewpoints will be based around your beliefs, this creates your reality! If you think you can't afford things, you will not attract wealth and prosperity, you will only attract poverty and mediocrity. The type of people you meet and situations, circumstances and events will support what you believe. Whenever you think about things you don't want, did you know that you are magnetizing what you don't want to you? You are creating your own hell! Focus on what you want! Attraction is the result of the vibration you are in.

If you have a great idea of something that you want to create and you get so emotionally involved in it. It will set up a vibration in your body and you will attract everything you need to make that idea become a reality. I will talk about my personal example in the chapter the laws at work. *"Everything moves, nothing rests".* This quote from Albert Einstein is to state that everything is in constant motion, everything is a frequency and at a rate of vibration. Nothing stands still although you may perceive it to. If you take a look at your hand underneath a microscope you will see that it is moving at a very rapid rate of vibration. Things around you may appear solid but they're not. They are moving so rapidly that they appear still to the naked eye. Have I just mind boggled you? If we go back to the law of attraction, I said that what we think about we attract. The thoughts or images we entertain are what causes an emotion in us. This feeling is what determines the rate of vibration that our bodies will vibrate. We are magnets so the rate of vibration will dictate what comes into our life. If you're at a low vibration, you have a bad feeling, if you are at a high vibration, you have a good feeling. Vibration is the foundation of the law of attraction.

FEELING IS VIBRATION

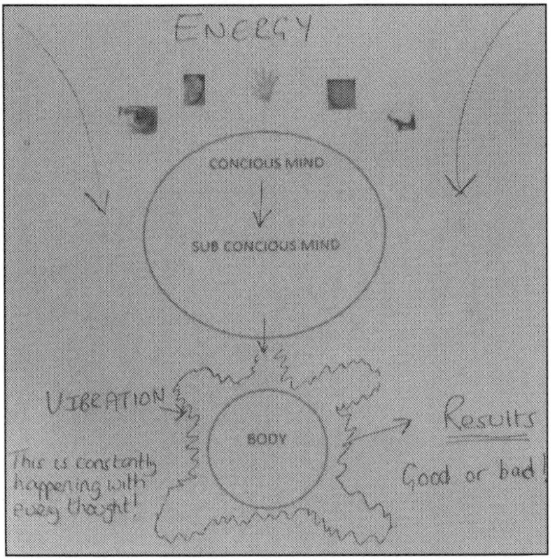

Change your feelings (vibration), you change what you attract. Samuell, how do I change my vibration you may ask? Good question, you change it by changing your thoughts, but not just your thoughts, it's a bit more complex than that. The aim is to change how you 'feel'. Feeling is emotion (energy in motion) and when you emotionally entertain an idea, it will alter the vibration causing you to act differently, thus changing what you attract.

YOU ATTRACT WHAT AND WHO YOU ARE IN HARMONY WITH, YOU SHARE THE SAME THOUGHTS AND FEELINGS AS THOSE YOU ARE IN HARMONY WITH.

There is a myth in the world that sad and hard times are normal -THAT IS A LIE! Abundance and happiness is your birthright. Anything else are false ideas, beliefs, and concepts that you accepted to be true and you are vibrating at that frequency, so by law you must attract sadness and hard times! The universe is unconditional. Perception comes into play here because no one or nothing can make you feel a certain way except for how you choose to view (perceive) what has happened or been said to you. Your intuition, which is a compilation of false or true ideas, is "judging" the experience you are having.

THE PROBLEM IS NOT OUTSIDE OF YOU, IT IS THE THOUGHT (SEED) THAT IS EVALUATING WHAT IS HAPPENING WHICH IS THE PROBLEM, NOT THE THING OR PERSON!

Sorry reader, but once you get this engrained in you it will save you so much stress, your thinking is the problem. If ideas are subconsciously accepted it MUST be a manifested reality for you. It was your CHOICE to ACCEPT the idea! Remember the stick figure person with the big head? That's you now, but that wasn't you when you first came here. When you were born, you had no conscious faculty developed, so your subconscious was wide open!!! Open for any and everything to be downloaded straight into it. Good or bad! Ask yourself:

What was the environment like that you lived in from birth to the age of 6?

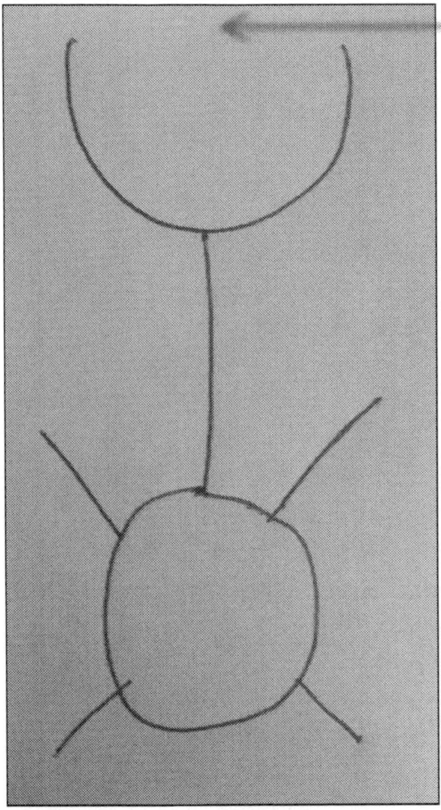

NO CONSCIOUS
FACULTY DEVELOPED

What were your parent's beliefs? What statements did you hear over and over again? Did you grow up in riches or poverty? Did you grow up in a healthy environment or a sick environment? Were you around motivated winners or demotivated failures? What foods did people in your environment eat, what did they feed you? What programs did you watch on TV? The list in endless but the lesson here is profound, all thoughts and information went straight into your subconscious and has a major impact on how you operate NOW!

Who would have imagined that a single thought from birth to the age of 6, would determine whether you were going to fail or win in life? Can you the reader see what may be holding you back? Can you see why you may not necessarily know why you do what you do? Where do your ideas come from? Who fed you what you currently believe? Take a close look at kids and their parents... you may have heard the saying *'the apple doesn't fall far from the tree'.* Children will only do what the parents do, children will believe what the parents show them or teach them *(irrespective of quality),* why? Because the subconscious is wide open and can only ACCEPT what it is given!

The amount of times I have seen mothers take their children somewhere and their baby is sleeping, and there is music playing where the lyrics and statements that are being said is not what a baby should be around, the fact that that baby is sleeping, it is absorbing everything in the environment including the songs that are being played. It's the same with having a child sleeping during parents watching films and TV, all that content goes straight into their child's subconscious and they have no idea! Why because parents don't know this information that is being taught here! Who can blame them?

Their parents didn't know either and it is a repetitive cycle that generations have gone through for years and years.

People wonder why they struggle moving forward and they blame people or circumstances, but if you look at everything you have just been taught it stems from thought, the question is when was that thought planted? *Most probably from birth to the age of 6...* I have personally on my journey been dissecting my thoughts and spending hours finding out why I do what I do? What I don't do what I want to do? Now I spend a lot of time changing my paradigm and reprogramming myself for success and wealth, so I can break the chain so my children do not inherit my ignorance and previous ancestry ideas of lack and failure, and the famous *"I can't do that"* attitude.

YOUR VIBRATION DICTATES WHAT YOU ATTRACT!

CHANGE YOUR THINKING CHANGE YOUR VIBRATION

NEW REALITY!
THIS IS THE PROCESS OF MANIFESTATION

LAW OF POLARITY

This law is something we touched on when we talked about perception. There are always two ends to a pole. Everything's an opposite. There are two sides to everything. We have a left and a right, an up and a down, a hot and a cold, a good and a bad, poor, and rich, do you get the picture? We cannot have one without the other. Everything just is! It's all one thing, just a different degree of vibration. Nothing is wrong or right, there are two sides to a story. If you picture a thermometer in your mind, tell me where hot starts? You can't, can you? Your hot might not be my hot, your cold might be my hot, and so there are two sides to the story.

If you look between each unit on a thermometer these are the different degrees, if you check the temperature of water, the water does not change it is the same, only a different degree of temperature or vibration. Can you see how this law links with the law of vibration? There's always another side, you cannot have a right without a left, there's no inside of something if there wasn't an outside, you cannot have an up with no down, everything just is. This last example may empower you when things get a little rough in your profession or study. If you say you can't do something there MUST be a way you can do it, why? That's the law of polarity. Unless your paradigm is making you think you can't...

What is making you think you can't? Its' your old conditioning and this is what cripples most of us, We were taught to fail so when a new idea comes to pass, we may easily reject it if we do not see that it 'fits' into what we think works or is classed as 'normal'. People sense of what's possible comes from what they think is possible, and what they think is possible comes from the information they receive to tell them what is possible, if you suppress the knowledge of what is possible, you suppress their perception of what is possible, and they will laugh in the face of the truth and say it's impossible, when actually if you understand to a greater level than the mainstream allows you to understand, you really not only realize it's possible but it's perfectlylogical...

Do you want an image? Do you remember as a child playing with a cube box with different shaped pegs (square, triangle, circle etc.)? Try banging a square peg (new idea) into a circle hole (your current knowledge), it doesn't fit, does it? So, what would you naturally do? You would reject it or make excuses saying, *"I can't do that!" "This isn't for me", "maybe next time", "it's impossible that can't happen"* ... do you get my drift reader?

IGNORANCE KNOWLEDGE

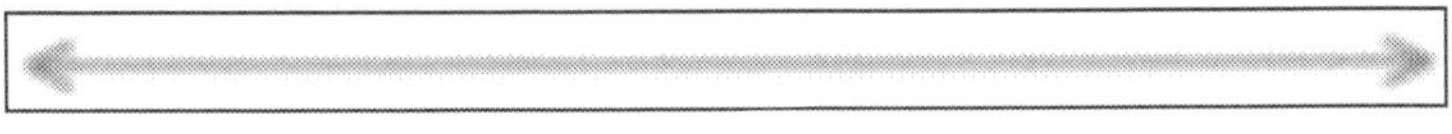

\- +

(Different degrees of Understanding)

Ignorance and knowledge are on either ends of a polarity scale, they are polar opposites. This is so simple but very misunderstood to a lot of people. When we put this law into perspective, we'll find out that it can have such a positive impact in people's lives as it will encourage them that it doesn't matter what may appear *'negative'* in their lives, there must be something *'right'* with it. Or if you *'can't'* do something there must be a reason you *'can'* do it.

LAW OF CAUSE AND EFFECT

This law just about sums up everything! This relates to Newton's law of action and reaction. Everything in life has its exchange. There's a cause and an effect and every effect is a cause. We are responsible for the causes that we put out; the effects take care of themselves. If you think back to the process of manifestation, it just about sums up cause and effect. Your thought is a cause, making your feeling an effect, this feeling is then a cause within itself, making the effect your action, and this action is then a cause that produces an effect for your result. Do you get the idea?

Everything is in constant motion, constant exchanges, and this law can be used to our advantage once we are aware of it. We are constantly causing and receiving the effects daily, I'm sure you have all heard of karma. It's the same principle; as you sow so shall you reap. Like causes produces like effects. Do good onto others and they will do good onto you and the same goes for the reverse. You may do someone wrong and think you'll get away with it but by law you must receive the effect whether it's the same day or next week. The good or wrong you do to somebody may not necessarily come back from those whom you serve, but it must come from somewhere because that is the law. A problem with a lot of people is that they expect effects without putting out causes. In relationships, we tend to wait for someone else to suit us (the effect) rather than we make the first step by giving (the cause). Your results in your life right now are in exact proportion to what you have caused. No one is to blame but you. Do you, the reader, understand this? My intention is not to annoy you but to awaken you to the realization of your responsibility in your life.

This is such an important law to understand, especially for those of you who are an example of a person who starts something and because you don't see results, you quit. Understanding leads to faith and with faith you will persevere. Remember the process of manifestation? Your big idea is a seed, it will become a reality if you allow it time to grow, but the problem most of us have is that you don't see results or anything happening that you class it as failure and you quit. This is so profound because we never question when a baby will be due because we *'understand'* there's a *'process'* before we see the result. It's the same principle. The key word here is *'understanding'*. Anything ispossible.

Take a look at a more detailed pic below of an acorn planted in the ground, *excuse my drawing as It's not my forte or strongest point for drawing.* Instantly and automatically it will attract particles of energy in the soil for it to grow, *bearing in mind that the acorn is very specific*, an entirely different seed could have been planted which would attract different particles of energy, because different seeds are on a different frequency or vibration, so it will attract like energy for its particular vibration.

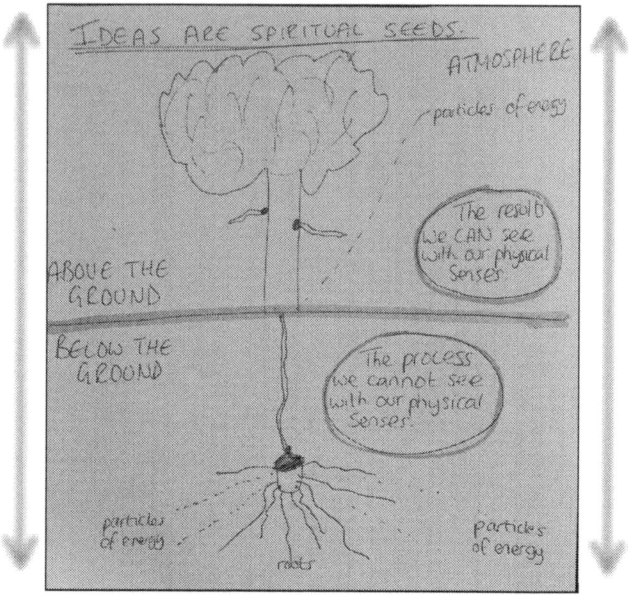

The acorn is a CAUSE and EFFECT within itself; it has a particular pattern that it must adhere to for its growth. In other words, it will attract whatever it needs from the earth for its enfoldment. If you add water on top of it, more and more will cause the acorn to expand and it will start to shoot roots and eventually, it will burst through the soil into the atmosphere where it will attract more energy from the outside, until eventually it has a trunk, branches and leaves and the whole thing.

This is metaphoric to our thoughts and ideas, it doesn't matter what quality of idea is in the soil it has an effect within it (good or bad) and it's only a matter of time before it is manifests. I mentioned in an earlier chapter that we don't see the process underneath, so if we didn't have this knowledge we wouldn't know if our ideas are working or not, so because we are impatient we would quit and therefore abort our ideas and say the classic phrase *"it didn't work" ... We as humans create the ideas and it becomes a nucleus and action taken and focus will make the nucleus expand and grow until eventually when it is time for it to be manifest it will show itself. DO NOT GIVE UP ON YOUR BIG IDEAS, DO NOT GIVE UP ON YOUR DREAMS, IT IS COMING!*

LAW OF RELATIVITY

All universal laws are related to each other. This law will help you to always look for the good in your situations. Nothing is ever good or bad, but your thinking makes it so. If you are going through a difficult time, you can relate it to somebody who is going through something worse and be grateful that your situation is not like his or hers. It's all about comparison, no one is either poor or rich, it just is. Nothings too big or small, it just is.

Your subconscious mind accepts anything you project onto it. It doesn't judge as we have already discussed, it doesn't know right from wrong or big from small. Everybody does something better than you but you must do something better than them. You can be poor and have better relationships or you could be rich with less healthier relationships. If you use this law correctly, you will always be in a constant state of gratitude. I'll give you an example, let's say you are a singer and you compare yourself to a top-class celebrity, you're not making it look good for yourself whereas if you relate yourself to someone less vocally developed than you, it makes you look better. Can you reader understand this? You can always build your self-esteem by using this law correctly. You make your situation seem what it is by virtue of how you use the law. Can you see how perception comes into this too? Start now by building a positive image of yourself and hold it in your mind and use the law of relativity to keep you feeling good and in a positive vibration. I must warn you though, don't just merely read these words.

LAW OF PERPETUAL TRANSMUTATION

Let's think back to the discussion of the mind where I showed you a diagram of the stick figure with a big head and showing the 5 senses above it. Everything we see, hear, taste, smell and touch together with our emotions is the manifestation of energy in various levels of vibration. Don't worry I'll explain, we all know we get energy from food that we eat. Each type of food has a different vibration and level of energy. Even the quality of information we accept from people, talks we get into is energy and it flows to and through us. Everything is moving in this universe and we move with it. The universe has its existence in an ocean of motion, 'change' is energy's only attribute and because of it comes all that is apparent to our material senses. It cannot be destroyed. Energy is in a constant state of transmission and transmutation. It is the cause and effect of any and everything. In other words, everything is constantly moving and changing. Energy *'just is'.*

Thought energy is non- physical and energy is spiritual. Look at the word: 'emotion'

E = MOTION

The "E" stands for energy, which equals motion, so energy is in motion. When we talk normally about emotion, little do we really understand it; we class emotions as angry, happy, sad etc. Whatever the emotion is, its energy. Remember polarity? Happy and sad are at either ends of the pole, the lower the vibration the sadder you feel, the higher the vibration the happier you feel. Whatever the ideas are in the subconscious mind causes the emotion. and it propels you to move and act out and in effect create the result. In other words, think back to the process of manifestation, this is exactly what the law entails. So, as it is with the universe where everything is constantly in motion. Non-physical forms of life are always moving into physical form. Thoughts are non-physical and when projected onto the subconscious mind, move to the physical where we do and act out the thing that was thought of. Do you the reader see behind the lines of what I am saying to you? Can you grasp it?

LAW OF RHYTHM

Rhythm is in everything, everything flows in and out, back and forward, up and down. When there's an advance there must be a retreat, something must rise when something sinks. Picture in your mind a weighing scale. If you put one weight in one end of the scale it will sink which will mean the other side rises. This law governs your mental, physical and emotional states. You at times feel good but then there are times you feel sad. It's like swinging a pendulum moving to one end and when it's ready it will swing to the other end. You wouldn't know what a good feeling was if you never experienced a bad feeling and vice versa. Our reason gives us the ability to choose our thoughts, where we can escape the swing of the pendulum to make us feel bad; we can choose to shift our thoughts to maintain a happy positive vibration. This is the only law that you can escape the effects of by using your reason mental faculty.

Remember it's all a perception. We have been conditioned to think that this thing called 'life' happens in a linear straight forward fashion. This is not so, because everything is in constant change which is changing how we are to operate in our lives. Once upon a time there was no social media but yet we have had to adapt to it through change. This has had to remove us from a paradigm of thinking while we keep up with the rhythms of this law. Look at every successful person, each person is a law unto him/herself which is why there is no set route to achieving whatever it is that we want. We as a people are connected, not separated. We are all working together whether we know it or not. Everyone has a part to play.

There's an intelligent synchronicity that is in constant motion in relation to your thoughts and ideas. Have you ever been in a situation where you had an idea, didn't know how you were going to achieve it but then something *strange* happened where you met someone who could help you or you discovered a piece of literature to read to aid you? These are only a couple of examples out of an infinite range of possibilities that the universe will make available for you. This is a good example of explaining the non-linear way of life where the ebbs and flow of RHYTHM will assist you.

LAW OF GENDER

I have to keep bringing the picture back to your mind regarding the process of manifestation. I'm sure by now you know this process deals with every aspect of your life. This law is one, which finally closes the cycle and completes the circle of the seven laws I have presented to you. It clearly shows you that the invisible creates the visible. Understanding of this law will empower you and misunderstanding will make you quit what you start. So, let's look at the positive only and help you to understand. We have already talked about the masculine and feminine duality aspect of the mind; hence the law is called gender, where creation happens once we have projected ideas from the conscious mind onto the subconscious. We know that thoughts create reality.

Look at this scenario: Jane set out to do something where she had her goals written out and she started moving in the direction she intended. After a while she got discouraged because she wasn't seeing any results, so she quit. What happened? She was unaware of the creative process, unaware of the law of gender. It takes time for ideas to become a reality. There's a time frame, remember all seeds have a gestation and incubation period. She didn't know that it was in creation; she didn't see the results in physical form, didn't see how it was going to happen so she quit. The answers she needed would have shown up for her but she decided not to go along with it anymore. What did Jane really need **KNOWLEDGE**

AND UNDERSTANDING OF THE LAWS! Remember, you cannot force a baby to grow you have to wait nine months, but you are aware that it is in progress. Do you understand? For any of you who want to go out there and do something, and work that powerful thing called the mind, if you have an idea and take action then it will be a reality, but bear in mind the law of gender. It takes time.

THE LAWS AT WORK

Ok, so we've discussed the laws and the mind, let's see how these laws work when we put it to use. All laws work in conjunction with one another. I am going to show you a real-life example of my own, explaining how everything comes together when you use the laws and act according to a true purpose. This will be by me repeating a section of my story and bringing in the laws so you can get a better understanding of how it works. December 2010 I had an idea that I wanted to create my own TV show, I had never done it before but I knew I wanted to do it. **THROUGH HAVING KNOWLEDGE OF THE LAWS,** it gave me confidence to step out of the box and do something different. By being an actor you get tired of waiting around for your agent to call you up with auditions and I knew I wanted more, I wanted to have something I could call my own, something I created that gave opportunities to other actors as well as help boost my name in the industry. I woke up one morning and I said to my little brother that I wanted to create my own show, I didn't know what but I wanted it to be funny. He told me that I should do it but I had no idea how to start. **AN IDEA WAS ORIGINATED IN MY**

CONCIOUS MIND THAT I GOT EMOTIONALLY INVOLVED IN.

The next day I paid a visit to my friend Arnold and we sat down with a sheet of paper for brainstorming. I was clueless as to what to start with so he said I should write a show about my life. I remember remaining silent and thought that it would be a great idea. After a couple of hours brainstorming I left confident knowing that with the notes we came up with I could come up with some characters. wrote down a goal and said by April 21st 2011 I would be in production. I didn't know how but that was my goal, I had something to worktowards. I knew the show I created had to be a hit, it had to be great. All I needed was a great script but I was unaware of how to go about doing it. I was researching how to go about writing a script professionally because I did not want to write it on Microsoft word. My whole attitude was to do everything the best of my ability so I looked up scripts from shows that had already aired and saw how the layout of their script was. They were all different but I knew I had to start somewhere so I chose one layout and began searching for some free scriptwriting software. How on earth could I start off writing a show?

One evening I was on my way to a seminar and I was on the bus and my brother text me. He said that my friend Ian had text him saying for me to call him. When I did we had a chat and he said that he was writing a script for his friend... I had known Ian for years but never knew he wrote scripts. This was the **LAW OF ATTRACTION** and **CAUSE & EFFECT** at work! We arranged to meet up one day so he could see where I was at with the idea. After spending a few hours with him we had come up with a plan for the first episode. I got straight to writing and about a week later I had written the first episode. The question was, now what? What was the next step? I didn't know. A week went by and I attended another seminar to see what was going on in social media. Someone approached me and recognized my face and introduced themselves to me. He asked me if I knew a person called Tony Adez in which I replied *"yes".* We got talking and he said that he saw Tony years ago editing my show-reel that's how he remembered my face. We exchanged details and I told him about what I was doing and he had a look at my script and said to me what I needed was a plan for future episodes. This is what I was lacking, a plan of how the show will pan out for the first series! I was meant to meet this person through the **LAW.**

I woke up one morning and was inspired by a thought to do a video presentation of my idea and put it online. This was so random but I knew that nothing was by accident according to knowing the laws. Spirit gave me an impression to take action on this presentation. I personally love doing video presentations they are fun. I thought this would be a great opportunity to let people know what I was doing and hopefully attract people that wanted to get involved. Without wasting anytime, I got out my laptop and loaded up PowerPoint and thought carefully how to construct the necessary slides to explain in detail what I was looking to do. As we think in pictures, it was wise to use pictures in the presentation so after looking at images on Google I found pictures of how I visualized the characters. I learnt how to use Adobe Photoshop to cut out the people in the pictures and combine them together through a lot of trial and error of course. After successfully completing this I knew that I wanted to record my voice narrating the presentation. I downloaded a free screen recording software and recorded myself talking about the project and stated at the end the type of people I were looking for and put my contact details on there.

A very *spooky* thing happened, the moment I had completed the presentation, my phone rang. It was the guy I met at the seminar! He asked me where I was at with my show and I told him about the presentation, he then suggested that I post it on a website called filmakersunited.com. I used my intuition and went along with it. 24 hours later a woman contacted me on the site saying my idea was very interesting. I had a look at her profile and saw a link to a website called starnow.co.uk. I never knew what this was but after some research I discovered that I could post on their site for free. It was this action, this **CAUSE** that had such a massive **EFFECT**. After posting it on the website, I had people contacting me every day via phone, email and Facebook wanting to get involved. In total, I had over 10,000 views and over 500 applications, I was so overwhelmed! People wanted to write, direct and act in the show.

To cut a long story short, I felt like a master of my life during the process because I was consciously creating my life and watching the miracles just happen in front of my eyes. You already know the rest of the story so I won't mention it again. Basically, I was walking by faith and not by sight. The more the good came my way the more confident I was and the more fear went out the window. Readers, I need you to understand that there is absolutely nothing to fear. When you are on purpose and passion, the universe will make things work for you but you must keep taking action. I'm not saying the ride was easy, believe me there were challenges and obstacles that I had to overcome, you read the whole story in the first section of this book! I had a director not show up, a writer who went AWOL. A filming location being denied to me in the middle of filming, an actress walking out of rehearsals saying she didn't want to be a part of it anymore, a cameraman turning up late and having my footage for two weeks without being contactable! This was only a few of the obstacles but I will not name everything, as I'm not looking to bore you with this story again.

The bottom line is from reading this segment of the story could you see the laws at work? Could you see where things started to happen as I carried on going forward? All because I was emotionally involved with an idea that I accepted into my subconscious mind. Could you see the creative process of **PERPETUAL TRANSMUTATION**? The next piece of the puzzle showed up every step I took. It was a scary, but exciting journey, and it's a journey I am still on up to this point in you reading this book... The question is now, what are you going to do and how are you going to use the laws to your advantage?

CHAPTER 12

WHAT DO YOU WANT?

We need direction, like actors need direction from a director. There must be a point of focus, a destination for where you are going in your life. If there is no direction you aren't going anywhere. As you've discovered from reading about the laws - it's all on you! Everything is cause and effect. What do you really want? *Seriously,* I never said what do you think you can have, I said WHAT DO YOU WANT?

You may look around and see everyone else being the star but you can be too! You can have anything you want! Don't worry what people say! Don't listen to people saying negative comments about you can't have this and that! Just remember you attracted this book and they didn't!

Wherever you are right now if you are not happy with your results you can change them.

If thoughts create our reality, then we all we need to do is change our thoughts then we will attract better things to us. I know this book is a lot to take in, and your mind may not agree with what is presented, but you now know that it is not you, it is your paradigm trying to keep you comfortable. Once you become aware of this paradigm that's the first step in change because you are now *aware* it is happening!

This is an infinite universe with unlimited possibilities and opportunities for everybody. Don't think there is not enough of this or that. There's an unlimited source of supply, the job you need is out there, the relationship you are looking for is out there but you need to change first, your thinking needs to change or else you will only attract the same kind of people, events, situations, and circumstances in your life. Grab a piece of paper, and write a 'want' list. List everything you want and be very specific, the universe loves specifics. Start the list off by saying 'I want...' then complete the sentence. There's no limit to how much you can write because you can have everything. This may seem too good to be true, but it is true, you just need to study it further. When you have written down what you want, when do you want to receive it by? Think when you would like to receive what you've asked for by, write a date down but think of realistic goals. Believe you will receive what you ask, and if you don't see any results along the way, remember just wait, need I remind you about the law of gender? Read through my example, and you will see that not everything happened all at once, there was a process, but do take note that I took steps to make it happen for myself, and the answers I needed showed up along the way as I was taking action. Energy in motion remember?

Get out of the thought process that you will wish and hope. You have to WILL and ACT to get what you want. Be the cause and the effect will show up, why? It's the law. Above all, show gratitude, be grateful for what you have now because if you are not grateful you shall not receive anything better, use the law of relativity and compare yourself to someone who's less fortunate and be happy. In all things give thanks. Send out those positive vibrations and start to treat people how you want to be treated. Keep doing this, then only good can happen to you. Now is the time to write down your life, after all... you do create it... you are the script writer...

CONCLUSION

So, there you have it, not your average book on acting, is it? Ironically enough, it does involve you having to 'act'. I wanted to share with you what can happen in your life when you make a firm decision to take charge of it. I started off just like you, an actor. I had achieved great gigs, however I questioned the status quo of roles, and made a decision to create my own show and unexpected things happened and I grew. Simultaneously, I was a student of the second half of this book. I kept feeding my mind this stimulating information and I attracted teachers, and certain literature and videos which aided my understanding.

Seeing as everything is a creation, we need to take heed to what actually shows up in our lives. Sometimes we might get into situations that are really horrible, believe me when I say that you created it. You are an energy centre and when energy is given out it returns to the source of where it came from (CAUSE AND EFFECT). I cannot stress the importance of taking control of your thoughts and guarding your mind from anything that does not relate to your purpose, vision, or goals. For those reading this book that are serious about taking charge of your lives and using this wonderful mind that you have, I strongly recommend further study into these laws and further study into the human mind. I have only touched on these laws; more depth is needed to understand.

I'd recommend purchasing my *'Thinking into Successful Results'* video series, as it gets more in-depth with this information where I will take you through everything I have mentioned in this second part to help you understand deeper. It's not a one off though you consciously need to study a bit more every day. Remember repetition of new information will shift the old paradigm that has kept you where you are up until now. You will know if your paradigm is keeping you comfortable when you start to make excuses for why you are not studying. This should make you aware of the power your paradigm has over you. Strong will power needs to be exercised for changing and transmuting your mind to think and act in a certain way.

You can have it all; you can live a fulfilling abundant life because that is what was intended from the beginning of time. I'm not saying it's a smooth road because it will take time for you to get to a consciousness where you have a deeper level of understanding where you will fear nothing and your intuition will be at a stage where you can literally read people like a book and you will feel like you are living in a completely different world. You will be at a higher vibration and higher state of consciousness where your closest friends and family will notice a change in the way you are. I must warn you some of these people will try their best to sway you from what you are doing by telling you that you are weird etc.

For your peace of mind, people thought Christopher Columbus was insane when he said the world wasn't flat but it was round; people thought Henry Ford was weird because he had an idea of something the world had not experienced which you now benefit from which is your car. The Wright brothers had an idea to make people experience flying in the sky; they too were looked upon as crazy. Do you get the idea? All these great inventors knew something that was beyond what society class as normal. They knew and believed in a higher existence outside all of us that governs every person, situation, circumstance, and event. This book was created for you to help you understand and become more aware of yourself, and your responsibility to your life and presence here on earth and to shine a light that there is nothing to fear, you can be the star, you can be the person you want to be, you can do what you want, why? Because YOU said so!

I'll tell you a few things that won't change. Night comes after day... I promise you that won't change, 24 hours a day... I promise you that won't change. You're going to be an extra year older next year... I promise you that won't change. What goes up must come down... I promise you that won't change. The only thing that can change is you and your thinking. So, start now!

Is your glass half full or half empty?

We are coming to the end of this book and there are three things I will mention to you. You can either:

1) Accept the information
2) Reject the information
3) Neglect the information

Due to the gift of free will you can do anything you want, but can I ask you something?

I'm asking you to 'evaluate' this information, if you feel it has been of any use to you then study this subject further. What I will say though, is that there is no accident you are reading this right now. You attracted this literature into your life and were meant to read this. The spiritual side of you has been prompting you to evolve and you needed this to aid you on our journey. Whether you like it or not, the fact that you have read this book up to the lines you are now reading has been a CAUSE, the EFFECT will take care of itself as the people, events and circumstances of life will manifest to provide you the next piece of the puzzle in *'understanding'.* I hope you have enjoyed this book as I have put my understanding and knowledge and experience into it over the course of 9 years, I have enjoyed compiling this info in a way you can grasp and visually see what I've presented. We think in pictures, with no picture, there's confusion. You may be new to the information in the second half of this book, and that's ok, if you want me to go over things in more depth, I have a video series that you can download where I teach you about this stuff to help you get more out of your life. Thank you for taking the time to read this book. I hope it helps you as it has helped me.

MORE PRODUCTS FROM THIS AUTHOR

A current list of services can be found at
www.SamuellBenta.Com

BOOKS/AUDIOBOOKS

- Why it's NOT ENOUGH to *just* be an ACTOR in the 21st Century
- A Black Actor's guide to SUCCESS in TV & Film in the 21st Century
- The Accidental TV Showrunner – How to *unconventionally* create your own TV show and CHANGE THE WORLD with YOUR VISION...
- Dear Young People – The RevoYOUtion is NOW!

VIDEO SERIES

- The Successful Young Men's Programme
- The Successful Young Women's Programme
- The Science of Self-Confidence
- The Metaphysics of Perception
- Thinking into Successful Results

ONLINE CLASSES

- The Successful Young Men's Programme
- The Successful Young Women's Programme
- The Science of Self-Confidence
- The Metaphysics of Perception
- Thinking into Successful Results

Made in the USA
Columbia, SC
27 July 2024

39494481R00162